D1433610

GRANDMOTHERS' LORE

GRANDMOTHERS' LORE

A Collection of Household Hints
from Past and Present

Simone Sekers

HODDER AND STOUGHTON
LONDON SYDNEY AUCKLAND TORONTO

British Library Cataloguing in Publication Data

Sekers, Simone
 Grandmothers' Lore

 1. Home economics — Great Britain
 I. Title
 640'.941   TX144

 ISBN 0 340 25303 7

Hodder and Stoughton Editorial Office: 47 Bedford Square, London WC1B 3DP.

❧ Contents ❧

The Kitchen   11

    Storage   13
    Preserving   17
    Baking   26
    Condiments   27
    Vegetables and Fruit   31
    Meat, Poultry and Game   32
    Hayboxes   34
    Cordials   36
    Culinary Hints   39
    General Hints   42

Household Work   45

    Furniture   47
    Floors   49
    Carpets and Rugs   51
    Cleaning Metals   55
    Fires   56
    General Hints   59
    Flowers, Fresh and Dried, for the House   70
    Pot-Pourri   74

Wardrobe and Laundry   78

    Dry Cleaning   80
    Stains on Non-washable Fabrics   82
    Laundering   83
    Dyeing   91
    Care of Clothes and Accessories   93
    Sewing   101

Out of Doors   107

Soil   109
Weeds   114
Planting   115
Companion Plants   117
Pests   117
Cuttings   120
Other Tips   121
Indoor Plants   124
The Weather   124
Animals and the Farmyard   127
Bees   132

Health   135

Infusions, Teas and Tonics   136
Health Drinks and Restoratives   140
Syrups   143
Ointments and Cures   145
First Aid   148
Preventives   159

Beauty   163

Lotions   165
Creams   168
Face Packs and Masks   171
Bath Condiments   172
General Beauty Tips   174

Custom and Superstitions   178

The Moon   180
The Calendar   181
The Home   182
The Garden   184
Magic Trees and Plants   185
Love   187
Baby Charms   188

Bibliography   191

ꙮ *Introduction* ꙮ

My own favourite books on housewifery were written between about 1650 and 1850 — efficient, and often bossy, but with a slow pace and thoroughness which gives the reader a sense of peace and order, a feeling of being at home. Those were the days when a house was not just a home, but a self-sufficient ship to be sailed through the seasons of the year, guided by a constellation of recipes for cheese-making, pig-keeping, poultry-rearing, brewing, sewing, cleaning, cooking and nursing. I have included many quotations from these books because besides their diverting nature, they are based on sound good sense.

Housewives and housework do not change greatly, although their aids have become mechanised. Gervase Markham, in 1615, describes the perfect housewife. She must be:

Chast of thoughts, stoutcourage, patient, untired, watchful, diligent, witty, pleasant, constant in friendship, full

7

of good Neighbourhood, wise in discourse, but not frequent therein, sharp and quick of speech, but not bitter or talkative, secret in her affairs, comfortable in her Counsels, and generally skilful in the worthy knowledges which do belong to her vocation.

If this seems a tall order, it is no more than the qualities needed today, when a housewife (now on her own, without a crew of housemaids, cooks and gardeners) often has to hold down a job and care for her family with a strong headwind of inflation blowing against her.

I have included hints for the housewife nearing shipwreck, and I hope they will be helpful. Many of them may seem obvious, but those are often the ones most easily overlooked. It is all too simple to apply a summer mulch zealously on a dry flower bed, or to spread manure happily over the vegetable garden so that 'the rain can wash the goodness in', only to find your plants perversely dying of thirst and a forest of strange weeds choking your beetroot and onions.

I enjoyed researching this book, although it has not made me a more diligent housewife — the windows still need cleaning, the garden remains undug, and we still reach for the aspirins and not the lavender drops to cure our headaches — but it has given me an insight into the galaxy of household tasks, and a greater interest and enjoyment in performing them. I do hope my readers will feel the same.

Simone Sekers, 1980

❧ *Conversion tables* ❧

WEIGHTS		
½ oz	10 g (grams)	
1	25	
1½	40	
2	50	
2½	60	
3	75	
4	110	
4½	125	
5	150	
6	175	
7	200	
8	225	
9	250	
10	275	
12	350	
1 lb	450	
1½	700	
2	900	
3	1 kg 350 g	

MEASUREMENTS	
$\frac{1}{8}$ in	3 mm (millimetre)
¼ in	½ cm (centimetre)
½	1
¾	2
1	2.5
1¼	3
1½	4
1¾	4.5
2	5
3	7.5
4	10
5	13
6	15
7	18
8	20
9	23
10	25.5
11	28
12	30

VOLUME

2 fl oz	55 ml	1¾ pints	1 litre
3 fl oz	75	4 gills (1 pint)	570 ml
5 fl oz (¼ pint)	150	2 pints (1 quart)	1.140 litre
½ pint	275	4 quarts (1 gallon)	4.560
¾ pint	425	2 gallons (1 peck)	9.120
1 pint	570	4 pecks (1 bushel)	36.480

All these are *approximate* conversions, which have been either rounded up or down.

9

❧The Kitchen❦

The modern kitchen would hardly be recognised as such by writers like Esther Copley, Eliza Acton or Mrs Beeton. The tiny space, compact as a ship's galley, walled in with cupboards from floor to ceiling, with a white and chrome cooker in place of the gleaming black range, bears little relation to the cavernous rooms of earlier days. Cooking itself has become more compact too, in some cases reduced to a simple movement from freezer to microwave oven. This is a pity because the kitchen should be the heart of the home and not the nerve-centre — a room big enough to be comfortable (though not so big that every meal entails a five-mile walk) as well as efficient. My favourite kitchens are mixtures of ancient and modern, the old advantages of separate larders and sculleries, the new ones of easy-care work surfaces and automatic cookers which do not depend on the direction of the wind for their temperature control.

One of the most welcoming rooms in English literature must be the kitchen to which John Clare's shepherd returns on a January evening:

> . . . as the warm blaze cracks and gleams
> The supper reeks in savoury streams
> Or kettle simmers merrily
> And tinkling cups are set for tea.
>
> *The Shepherd's Calendar*

Many of the cottage kitchens in this village, and throughout the North, still present similarly cosy pictures. The delicious smell wafting from back doors and windows between 5.30 and 6 indicate that high tea is alive and well; baking day is still Friday for many of our neighbours, and the Sunday roast continues to cast its post-prandial somnolence over the allotments on which most of the accompanying vegetables are grown. But only a few miles away, microwave ovens are interfering with the radio-telescope at Jodrell Bank — another world, another era.

Personally, I do not mourn the pasing of kitchen staff, not only because I enjoy all the aspects of cooking too much to want to relinquish them, but also because of the delicate tightrope of tact the mistress of the house had to walk with her cook, who is so often portrayed as a difficult and temperamental character. Esther Copley describes the harmony that could result in a well-run establishment:

> It is astonishing how much may be saved both to mistress and servant, if the former, before leaving the kitchen, can intimate to the latter what is likely to be wanted on the ensuing day; Orders may then be given to the butcher and gardener; provisions sent in in the cool of the morning, and ready for the superintending directions of the mistress immediately after breakfast. A ham, if required, may be

put in soak overnight, and the copper lit early in the morning; plums and currants may be cleaned and picked for a pudding — and indeed if the pudding is made the day previous to its being wanted, the ingredients will be the more thoroughly incorporated.

The Housekeeper's Guide, 1834

This does present a wonderful scene of peace, order and plenty, and it would be pleasant to be able to copy some aspects — the vegetables being brought to the kitchen door by the gardener, the ham which once hung from the larder ceiling being lifted down and left to soak overnight before being simmered in the copper. But the piles of sticky dried fruit which had to be laboriously stoned, and the 'superintending directions' which must have been almost as arduous as the tasks themselves, belong to the days of smoking ranges, fly-blown meat (no refrigerators), and flour full of weevils. We certainly have much to be thankful for.

❧ *Storage* ❧

Vegetables will keep best on a stone floor if the air be excluded — Meat in a cold, dry place — Sugar and sweet-meats require a dry place, so does salt — candles cold but not damp — Dried meats, hams, etc the same — All sorts of seeds for puddings, saloop, rice, etc should be close covered to preserve from insects; but that will not prevent it, if long kept. Earthen pans and covers keep it (bread) best. Straw to lay apples on should be quite dry, to prevent a musty taste. Large pears should be tied up by the stalk.

A New System of Domestic Cookery, 1818

To keep bread fresh, store it with a well-scrubbed, dry potato in the bin.

To keep cake fresh, keep an apple in the tin.

Do not store eggs in the fridge. If you are short of space, a wall-hung wooden egg-rack looks decorative and keeps the eggs at the right temperature for cooking. Always store them pointed-end down, so that they keep longer.

Left-over egg yolks, if still whole, keep quite well for a day or two in the fridge, if they are covered with about ½ in cold water to stop them drying out. If they have broken, beat them up with a teaspoon of water, and cover the bowl with cling-wrap.

To store a whole cheese, cut a thin slice off the top and butter the underside. Use this as a lid and replace it each time the cheese is used. Keep the cheese in a cool place, but preferably not in the fridge. This tip was given to me by a Cheshire farmer, and although we were discussing Blue Cheshire cheese at the time, it applies to all whole cheeses. Old cookery books also advise wrapping the cheese in a damp muslin cloth, changed frequently; this is a good idea in the summer, but not really necessary in the winter.

Milk keeps quite well in hot weather if wrapped in wet newspaper. The newspaper should never be allowed to dry out. This is a useful tip if you find yourself without a fridge.

Wrap raw meat loosely and keep it away from cooked food in the fridge. This is particularly important with poultry.

Remove the giblets of a fresh chicken and put an onion in the cavity instead, to keep it fresh. Cook the giblets before the chicken, if necessary, as they keep less well.

To keep a hare a long Time

As soon as it is killed and discharged of its Entrails, take care that all the Blood be dried away with Cloths about the Liver, for there it is apt to settle, then dust the Liver well with Pepper, and fill the Body with Nettles or dry Moss; for these will not raise a ferment, as Hay and Straw will do, when they come to be wet; then fill the Mouth with Pepper and it will keep a long time.

The Country Housewife, 1753

This is my mother-in-law's tip for storing a whole salami: once it has been cut, cover the sliced end with cling-wrap and hang it in an airy place, cut-end down, so that the fat in the rest of the sausage runs down to stop the cut side becoming dry.

Do not put a joint away on the plate on which it was carved, as the juices will sour very quickly and turn the meat bad.

Allow the steam to escape from hot food before putting it away, or the condensation will make it go bad very quickly. Draw the lid to one side until the food has cooled, then replace it.

Spices and dried herbs should be stored away from air *and* light. Old Bovril and Marmite jars are ideal containers, or any of the black japanned-tin boxes which can sometimes be found in junk shops. Small cotton bags made with a draw-string top and the name of the herb written on with a marker-pen are a very convenient method of storage if you are short of space, as they can be hung on a hook near the cooker, and washed easily when necessary.

Dried bay leaves will keep better if stored in an air-tight container with a piece of cotton rag dipped in olive oil.

To stop salt from becoming lumpy, mix 1 heaped tablespoon of cornflour thoroughly with each pound of salt. Adding a few grains of rice to salt in a shaker will keep it dry and free-running.

Seville oranges can be stored in the freezer until you have time to make your marmalade. Pack them in polythene bags, tying the neck firmly. I have tried freezing them without putting them in bags first, but they do dry out a little and become less juicy. I keep some back from marmalade-making to use in sauces for duck and pork, and even fish. They unfreeze very quickly.

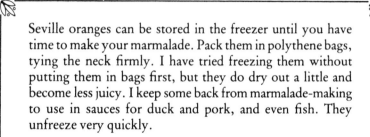

Preserving

To Salt Runner Beans

Pick the beans on a dry day while they are young and small (about 6 in long), and break them into approximately 1 in lengths — don't shred them. Pack the pieces into a glass or stoneware jar in layers about 2 in deep, covering each layer with a generous sprinkling of kitchen salt. When the jar is full, cover it with waxed paper or polythene held down with a rubber band — metal lids would be corroded by the salt.

To use the beans, soak them in cold water for about an hour before cooking as usual.

To make Sprats taste like Anchovies

Salt them well and let the salt drain from them. In 24 hours wipe them dry, but do not wash them. Mix 4 oz of common salt, 1 oz of bay salt, 1 oz saltpetre, ½ oz of sal-prunel and half a teaspoon of cochineal, all in the finest powder. Sprinkle it among 3 quarts of the fish, and pack them in two stone jars. Keep in a cold place, fastened down with a bladder. These are pleasant on bread and butter, but use the best for sauce.

A New System of Domestic Cookery, 1818

A good recipe to try when sprats are very cheap. Substitute sea salt for 'bay salt'. 'Sal-prunel' was a variety of saltpetre, so use 1½ oz saltpetre instead. Cochineal is included presumably to give the sprats the same pinkish colour as anchovies, so that it can be left out, if you like.

Saltpetre is sometimes difficult to buy, but if you have a friendly dispensing chemist you should be able to explain to him that you want it for culinary purposes and not as an explosive!

Eggs — To Preserve for Winter Use
For every 3 gallons of water, put in 1 pint of fresh slaked lime, and common salt from 1–2 pints; mix well and let the barrel be about half full of this fluid, then with a dish let down your eggs into it, tipping the dish after it fills with water, so they roll out without cracking the shell, for if the shell is cracked the eggs will spoil. If fresh eggs are put in, fresh eggs will come out, as I have seen men who have kept them two, and even four, years at sea.

Dr Chase's Recipes, c. 1880

If you can collect new-laid eggs, rub them all over with a butter-wrapper before putting them away. This seals the air out of the porous egg shell and will preserve their new-laid flavour a little longer.

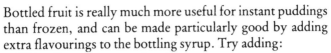

Bottled fruit is really much more useful for instant puddings than frozen, and can be made particularly good by adding extra flavourings to the bottling syrup. Try adding:

    Elder-flowers to gooseberries
    Cinnamon sticks and cloves to damsons
    Grated orange peel and brown sugar to rhubarb
    Madeira or sweet sherry to plums
    Currant leaves to the currants themselves, black, white
        or red
    A vanilla pod to apricots

My tried and tested bottling method is as follows:

Make a syrup of 8–12 oz sugar per pint of water (depending on the acidity of the fruit to be bottled), adding extra flavourings as above. Simmer the syrup for about 20 minutes, then cool. Fill Kilner jars with washed and drained fruit to within 1 in of the top, then pour on the syrup to come to the brim. Put on the Kilner lids, but not the screw bands, and stand the jars without touching each other in a large roasting-tin half filled with hot water. Put the tin and jars low in a pre-heated oven at 325°F, 160°C, Gas Mark 3, and leave for 1½–2 hours, until the fruit is seen to be soft. Take the jars out and stand them on thick newspaper in a cool place, screwing on the screw bands tightly. As each seal 'takes', a loud 'pop' will be heard. To test for sealing, remove the screw bands and pick each jar up by the Kilner lid alone; if this holds, the seal is effective and the fruit can be stored for at least 4 years. If it does not, you can either repeat the process from the stage where you put the jars in the oven, with fresh lids, or you can give in and freeze the contents of the jar.

To Dry Damsons

Get your damsons when they are full ripe, spread them on a coarse cloth, set them in a very cool oven, let them stand a day or two; if they are not as dry as a fresh prune, put them in another cool oven for a day or two longer, till they are pretty dry, then put them out, and lay them in a dry place; they will eat like fresh plums in the winter.

The Experienced English Housekeeper, 1794

The recipe works well for plums, too. The bottom oven of an Aga or something similar is obviously ideal for this method.

To dry your own herbs, pick them on a dry day when the sun has dried the dew, and before the plants themselves come into flower. Dry them between sheets of newspaper in the airing cupboard, rub the leaves from the stems and store them in one of the ways suggested on page 16. Be ruthless about throwing away herbs which are more than about a year old, as they will just add a musty flavour to the food; bay leaves are the exception (see page 16).

A war-time method of drying parsley:

Bring 1 pint water and 2 teaspoons bicarbonate of soda to the boil. Make bunches of the parsley sprigs, tying each bunch with a length of string. Hold each bunch upside down in the boiling water by the string for 1 minute. Shake well, untie the bunch and spread the sprigs on a cake-rack, then dry them out in a low oven. Pack them loosely in an air-tight box, and soak for 15 minutes in cold water before using. Of

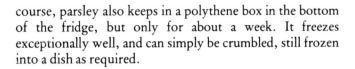

course, parsley also keeps in a polythene box in the bottom of the fridge, but only for about a week. It freezes exceptionally well, and can simply be crumbled, still frozen into a dish as required.

To Candy Flowers with their own colours:

Take Gum Arabick and steep it in Rose-water all night. The next day take what flowers or Herbs you please and dip them well in that Gum water and swing them well from it, then strew them very thick with Sugar beaten fine on every side, and lay them upon plates to dry in the sun, and when you find they begin to dry, turn them on clean plates, and if you find sugar wanting, supply it.

The Compleat Gentlewoman

Primroses, violets, single roses, single pinks, and the leaves of lemon balm, bergamot, sweet cicely and wild strawberries are among the best flowers and leaves for candying. Gum arabic and rose water are both available from good chemists. Dissolve about 1 oz gum in 5 fl oz rose water. Dip the flowers in this, shake them, then dip them in caster sugar and dry them on a cake-rack in the airing cupboard. Store them in an air-tight box. They make very pretty cake and pudding decorations, which children love being able to eat.

Economy Lemon Curd
This is a war-time recipe and very good.

2 lemons	1 cup sugar
2 eggs	2 teaspoons cornflour
2 cups water	1 oz margarine

Grate the lemon peel into a saucepan with the sugar and water. Mix the cornflour with the lemon juice and stir it in, then cook over a low heat until thickened. Beat the eggs well, remove the pan from the heat and beat the eggs into the lemon mixture. Return to the lowest heat for a minute or two, but don't allow the mixture to boil or the eggs will curdle.

Lemon Pickle

6 large lemons
6 large cloves garlic
1 lb kitchen salt
2 oz fresh horseradish
2 oz dried mustard
Nutmeg, mace, cloves and cayenne to taste

Peel the lemons thickly to remove as much pith as possible. Cut them in half, then in quarters, then cut each quarter in half horizontally. Peel and dice the horseradish, and slice the garlic. Mix all the ingredients together, adding the spices to suit your own taste. Stand for 24 hours until the salt has dissolved, then boil up the pickle for 15 minutes. Put it into a stoneware or glass jar and leave it to stand for a fortnight, stirring daily. Pot and cover with waxed paper or plastic.

This pickle is very good with curries.

To stop jam burning, either drop a 10p piece into the preserving pan, or rub the pan with butter before putting in the

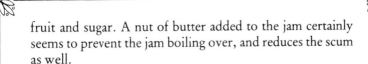

fruit and sugar. A nut of butter added to the jam certainly seems to prevent the jam boiling over, and reduces the scum as well.

To test jam for setting

After the first 10 minutes of fast boiling, pull the pan off the heat and drop a little jam on a cold saucer. A skin will form very quickly if the jam is ready, and will wrinkle if pushed with a fingertip. If this does not happen, return the pan to the heat and boil for one minute before testing again. If it is still not ready, boil for another 10 minutes before testing once more.

To stop fruit rising to the top of the jam in the jar, withdraw the pan from the heat when setting point is reached and leave it to stand for about 15–20 minutes. Stir the jam thoroughly and then pot it.

Having had several batches of jam which went mouldy very quickly, I now make sure that the jam jars are not only warm and clean when I pot the jam, but absolutely dry as well.

Economy Jam

This recipe uses very little sugar, and the jam has a good flavour.

    4 lbs soft fruit (raspberries, red or white currants)
    2 lbs sugar
    1 teaspoon salt

Cook the fruit until soft, add the sugar and salt and bring to the boil. Boil fast for 10 minutes and test for setting, then, when ready, pot in warm, dry jars and seal.

Mock Apricot Jam

    6 sweet oranges
    2 lbs rhubarb
    4 lbs sugar
    A handful of blanched almonds

Cut the rhubarb into pieces. Grate the rind of one orange and peel and slice the rest, including the one with the grated orange rind. Cook the fruit and the grated rind until soft, then add the sugar and boil for 10 minutes. Test for setting and, when ready, stir in the almonds and pot.

Not much like apricots, but very pleasant and useful if you have large crops of rhubarb.

Freezer Jam

    2 lbs soft fruit
    1 lb caster sugar

Mash the fruit with the sugar and leave to stand overnight. Next day, liquidise and pour into small, clean jars — mustard jars are about the right size — leaving a gap at the top so that the jam can expand while freezing.

This is extremely useful for winter puddings: heat it as a sauce for ice cream, pancakes or steamed sponge puddings, or whisk egg whites into it to make a sorbet. Baked apples are good if surrounded with the jam as they bake. It defrosts quickly and a jar will keep for at least a fortnight in the fridge once unfrozen.

Pressure-cooker Marmalade

12 Seville oranges
2 lemons
1 lb sugar per pint of jam (see recipe)
A nut of butter

Put the fruit in a pressure cooker with 2 pints of water. Bring to pressure, then cook for 25 minutes. Reduce pressure at room temperature. Halve the fruit and scoop the pith and pips into a bowl. Cut up the peel — either chop or slice, depending on your preference — and put it in a large bowl, together with the water in which the fruit was cooked. Sieve the pulp and add to the peel and water, together with another 3 pints of cold water. Leave for 24 hours. Measure the whole before putting it in a preserving pan rubbed with butter, bring it to the boil and add 1 lb sugar for each pint. Cook for approximately 35 minutes, or until the setting point is reached. Pot in warm, dry jars and seal. Makes about 10 lbs.

This is a marvellous recipe, both from the point of view of fuel-saving, and because the marmalade itself is very good. Sadly, I cannot remember who gave it to me; it was at least twelve years ago. I have made it every year since then and I am deeply grateful for it.

Cherries and strawberries are both low in pectin, and to help the jam set you can either add the juice of one lemon to every

3 lbs of fruit, or you can make your own pectin from apples if you have a large crop.

Apple Pectin

Fill a pan with roughly-chopped apples; there is no need to peel and core them. Add water to cover them and simmer until the fruit is soft, then strain through a jelly-bag (or an old pillowcase). Re-heat the juice to boiling point and pour it into warm, dry Kilner jars, putting on the lids and screw bands immediately. Provided the seal takes, this can be stored indefinitely. Add ½ pint to 1 lb fruit and ¾ lb sugar.

Rowan jelly goes well with game, lamb and pork; it has a delicious bitter and slightly smoky flavour. Use any jelly recipe to make it, and add some of the above apple pectin if you want a firm set, as rowans are low in pectin and the jelly does not set firmly. This jelly improves with keeping.

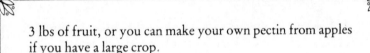

Baking

Put a shallow dish of cold water in the bottom of an oven to stop cakes from burning. This is particulary useful when leaving a rich fruit cake to cook unattended, and it also seems to help produce a moister cake.

If you are short of eggs when making a rich fruit cake, at least one egg can be replaced with a tablespoon of vinegar. Surprisingly, it adds a very good flavour to the cake.

Stop the cherries sinking to the bottom of a cherry cake by adding a pinch of cream of tartar to the flour.

Baking Powder
Put 3 oz baking soda and 4 oz cream of tartar on a sheet of greaseproof paper in a low oven until warmed through. Mix thoroughly and store in a polythene bag in a screw-top jar.

Mix pastry to be served cold with milk rather than water; it will be crisper.

As all fuel is now so expensive, always try to fill the oven if you have it on, cooking vegetables in roasting-bags with butter and herbs as you roast a joint, or baking a fruit cake while you cook a casserole.

Dishes which need long, slow cooking can be started in a cold oven, thus making use of all the heat. Joints and poultry should, of course, be put into a pre-heated oven to seal them.

❧ Condiments ❧

Browning for Made Dishes
Beat small 4 ounces of treble-refined sugar, put it in a clear frying-pan with 1 ounce of butter, set it over a clear fire,

mix it very well together all the time; when it begins to be frothy, the sugar is dissolving, hold it higher over the fire, have ready a pint of red wine; when the sugar and butter is of a deep brown, pour in a little of the wine, stir it well together, then add more wine, and keep stirring it all the time; put in half an ounce of Jamaica pepper, six cloves, four shalots peeled, two or three blades of mace, three spoonfuls of mushroom catchup, a little salt, the out-rind of one lemon; boil it slowly for 10 minutes, pour it into a basin; when cold take off the scum very clean, and bottle it for use.

The Experienced English Housekeeper, 1794

This is the most delicious gravy browning recipe I have found, and is really quite quick to make. Jamaica pepper is allspice. I chop the shallots, and strain the sauce before bottling it.

Eliza Acton's 'Brown Flour for Thickening Soups and Gravies'

Spread it on a tin or dish, and colour it without burning in a gentle oven . . . turning it often, or the edges will be too much browned before the middle is enough so. This, blended with butter, makes a convenient thickening for soups or gravies, of which it is desirable to deepen the colour, and it requires less time and attention than the French *roux*.

Modern Cookery for Private Families, 1845

Use it in conjuction with the previous recipe for browning, to make very superior sauces and gravies.

Table Pepper

½ lb white pepper	1 oz mace
1 oz nutmeg	1 oz cayenne pepper

Mix all the ingredients and fill the cruets.

This is a sixty-year-old recipe from Carlisle. It also makes a very good seasoning for use when making pâtés.

Try making up mustard with sherry when serving it with roast beef or steak and kidney pie.

Aromatic Herbaceous Seasoning

Take of nutmegs and mace 1 oz of each; of cloves and peppercorns 2 oz each; 1 oz dried bay leaves, 3 oz dried basil, the same of marjoram, 2 oz winter savoury, 3 oz thyme, ½ oz of cayenne, the same of grated lemon peel, and 2 cloves of garlic; all these ingredients must be well pulverised in a mortar and sifted through a fine wire sieve, and put away in dry corked bottles for use.

The Cook's Guide, 1888

This is a very good seasoning for stews, particularly oxtail, and for jugged hare. I put all the ingredients in the blender, then dry them off in a low oven on a baking-sheet so that the garlic and the lemon peel don't go bad. Store in an old Marmite jar.

To make Gooseberry Vinegar

Take the ripest gooseberries you can, crush them with your hands in a tub. To every peck of gooseberries put 2 gallons

of water, mix them well together and let them work for 3
weeks. Stir them up three or four times a day, then strain the
liquor through a hair sieve, and put to every gallon a pound
of brown sugar, a pound of treacle, a spoonful of fresh barm
[yeast], and let it work three or four days in the same tub
well washed. Run it into iron-hooped barrels and let it stand
12 months, then draw it into bottles for use. This far exceeds
white wine vinegar.

The Experienced English Housekeeper, 1794

Herb Vinegars

Tarragon: Put 2–3 large sprigs of bruised tarragon into a
   bottle of white wine, or cider vinegar.
Celery: Put a handful of well-washed leaves into a bottle of
   cider vinegar.
Garlic: Crush 4 large cloves of garlic lightly and add them to
   white wine vinegar.
Basil: Red wine vinegar is best for this and for the next two
   herbs, marjoram and thyme, as all three have warm, spicy
   flavours.
   Proceed as above.
   All the vinegars should be stored for at least a month
before using. The tarragon and celery vinegars are very good
in fish recipes, especially in *court bouillons*. Add the garlic
vinegar to curries, and the red wine vinegars to winter stews
and brown soups. Try mixing two together in a salad
dressing: garlic and basil for tomatoes, celery and thyme for
mushrooms, tarragon and marjoram for cucumber, etc.

If you are using an orange or lemon just for its juice, grate
the rind first, and let it dry out in a low oven. Store it in a
small jar, where it will be ready for use as a flavouring.

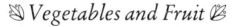 Vegetables and Fruit

Add a handful of salt to the water in which you are peeling root vegetables, to prevent your hands getting stained.

Peeling onions from the root end first will stop your eyes watering. If peeling onions in any quantity, peel them under water in a bowl, with the cold tap running into the bowl all the time. This is a very useful tip to remember when making pickled onions.

When cooking brassicas of any sort, add a teaspoonful of sugar to the water to help stop the smell. A slice of bread, tied in a pudding-cloth, absorbs the smell of cooking cauliflower; put it on top of the cauliflower in the pan.

A simple rule to remember when cooking vegetables: cook underground (root) vegetables with the lid *on*, and green vegetables with the lid *off*.

Add a pinch of baking powder to potatoes when mashing them to make them lighter. This is economical, but plenty of butter and milk make the lightest and nicest mashed potatoes.

Potatoes take less time to bake if they are soaked for 15 minutes in hot water first. A metal skewer through each one also cuts down on the baking time, as the heat is conducted through the potato by the metal. You can buy special gadgets for this, but skewers are easier to clean and can be used for so many other things.

Derbyshire Baked Potatoes for High Tea

Bake large, floury potatoes. When they are done, make a hole in the top of each and mash up the insides with a fork, together with a large lump of salty butter, pepper and a little nutmeg. Tie a napkin round each, stick a teaspoon in each potato, and serve with a jug of cream to pour in the top. Very fattening, comforting, and absolutely delicious, especially after a long cold walk.

When cooking acid fruit, such as gooseberries or rhubarb, add a few stalks of sweet cicely; you will need to use far less sugar.

꩜ Meat, Poultry and Game ꩜

To hang a Surloin of Beef to Roast

Take the suet off a surloin, and rub it half an hour with one ounce of saltpetre, four ounces of common salt, and half a pound of brown sugar. Hang it up 10 or 12 days, then wash it and roast it; you may eat it either hot or cold.

The Experienced English Housekeeper, 1794

A delicious and useful recipe, especially if you have no freezer. Quarter the above amounts of salt, sugar and salt-petre for the average-sized joint nowadays.

To test feathered game, pull out a feather just above the tail. If it comes out fairly easily, the bird is well hung enough for most tastes.

Hang game birds up by the neck, and hares up by the back legs.

Dip poultry in boiling water before plucking to loosen the feathers. Friends who keep hens say this helps enormously, but that unfortunately it doesn't work for birds with water-repellent plumage.

Meat that has been left in its wrappings too long, and which smells stale, can be rubbed over with diluted vinegar to freshen it before cooking. Make sure that the meat itself has not gone off.

To make good pork dripping
Buy fresh back pork fat from the butcher (or he may even give it to you). Melt it very slowly in a *low* oven, or over a

very low heat, with a sprig of rosemary in the pan. Pour the melted lard into a pudding basin and add two more sprigs of rosemary.

Dripping treated in this way was 'cottagers' butter', made from the fat of their own pig and flavoured with the rosemary to be found growing in almost every cottage garden. It is delicious on hot toast, and gives a wonderful flavour to fried potatoes, or to any meat or vegetables browned in it.

To make pork crackling crackle, rub the skin with salt and olive oil before putting the joint in the oven, and put the meat on a rack so that it will be crisp all round. A loin of pork produces the best crackling, as it has a thicker layer of fat beneath the skin than either leg or shoulder.

Add a spoonful or two of water to stop fat in a roasting-tin burning — it will help the gravy, too.

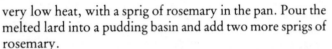

🌿 *Hayboxes* 🌿

Now that electrically-operated slow cookers are available, it may seem superfluous to give tips on hayboxes. However, provided you have enough room to accommodate one, they have one or two advantages over a slow cooker, the most obvious being that of cheapness, both to make and run.

To make a haybox you will need a wooden box — a small tea-chest is ideal — hay (or, if you cannot get hold of any, polystyrene granules will do very well instead), 6 large polythene sacks and 6 old pillowcases. Fill the sacks generously with hay or granules, and fasten the tops with staples or sellotape. Slip each filled sack into a pillowcase and fit these round the inside of the chest, making sure that there are no corners where heat might escape.

Start your soup, stew, porridge, milk pudding, in the usual way, letting it reach boiling point, then simmering it for at least 20 minutes before putting it in the haybox to finish cooking. It is most important that the food should cook for some time at a high enough heat to kill any organisms which might be present, particularly if you are cooking a frozen chicken. A stew put in at breakfast time should be ready for supper, porridge made in the evening will be ready for breakfast (porridge fanatics say that haybox porridge is the best of all).

Haybox Porridge
For every two people, bring ½ pint lightly salted water to the boil. Sprinkle 2 oz medium oatmeal on to the water, stirring briskly with a wooden spoon to avoid lumps. When the porridge is boiling, turn off the heat, lid the pan tightly and put it in the haybox, put on the cover and the lid and leave overnight.

Ham Hot-Pot

This is a recipe from Mungrisedale in Cumbria, and is another ideal haybox dish.

    1 lb ham, left over from a ham joint
    1 lb potatoes, peeled and sliced
    2 Cox's apples, peeled, cored and sliced
    1 onion, chopped
    1 dessertspoon brown sugar
    1 tablespoon mushroom ketchup
    Hot stock, to cover

Layer the ham, potatoes, apples, onion and sugar in a casserole, seasoning each layer with salt and pepper, and ending with a layer of potatoes. Sprinkle the ketchup on top, and pour on enough hot stock (ham stock, if you have it) to come level with the top of the ingredients. Bring to the boil, simmer for 10 minutes (as the meat is already cooked), then put it in the haybox and leave it all day. About 10 minutes before serving, brown the top under the grill.

❧ *Cordials* ☙

Parson Woodforde's Mead

Monday, Oct. 20th, 1794: Busy most part of the Afternoon in making some Mead wine, to fourteen Pound of Honey, I put four Gallons of Water, boiled it more than an hour with Ginger and two handfulls of dried Elder-flowers in it, and skimmed it well. Then put it into a Small Tub to cool, and when almost cold I put in a large gravy-spoon full of fresh Yeast, keeping it in a warm place, the Kitchen during night.

The Diary of a Country Parson

Windfall Cider

Wash small windfall apples, cut out any rotten bits and chop the apples roughly. Put them in a deep container — a plastic beer fermentation bucket is very good — and cover the apples with cold water. Cover the bucket with a cloth and leave for about 10 days, stirring daily. When fermentation, which is not all that vigorous, has stopped, strain the cider and add 1¼ lb sugar to each gallon. Return the cider to the bucket and leave another fortnight, without stirring. When the cider has ceased working, bottle it and cork the bottles — do not use screw caps. In about 3 months the cider should be clear and sparkling and ready to drink.

Hawthorn Cordial

Fill a Kilner jar with fully-opened hawthorn flowers picked on a dry day. Cover with brandy, put a lid on the jar and leave for 3 months. Sweeten it to taste with a syrup made by boiling 12 oz sugar for 15 minutes in 1 pint water. Strain the cordial, bottle it and keep another month before drinking.

Somerset Boatmen's Punch

Put a poker to heat in the fire, and pour 1 pint of cider (real 'scrumpy' if you can get it), into a metal tankard. Grate ginger on top of the cider, and make some toast as the poker is heating. When the poker is red hot, plunge it into the cider and leave it until the punch is hot. Take out the poker and scatter pieces of broken toast on top. Bracing, sustaining and exciting to make.

A Harvest Drink

This is not unlike lemon barley water and is very refreshing.

4 oz fine oatmeal	2 sliced lemons
6 oz sugar	4 pints boiling water

Put the oatmeal, sugar and lemons in a large pan. Mix together with a little warm water, then pour on 4 pints of boiling water. Stir thoroughly and leave to cool. Strain, bottle and store in a cool place.

This was taken into the fields by the workers at harvest time, and is a very effective thirst-quencher.

Lemon Honeyade

3 lemons	1½ pints water
6 tablespoons honey	Ice and mint

Squeeze the lemons and stir the honey into the juice and add the water. Strain over ice in tall glasses and garnish with mint.

Although meant as a summer drink, it is also very good for anyone in bed with 'flu.

Lucy's Summer Drink

Fill a wide-mouthed bottle with water, and add plenty of fresh mint, and a strip each of cucumber and lemon peel. Re-make every day.

My daughter makes up a bottle of this and keeps it in the fridge, finding it more refreshing in hot weather than sticky fruit drinks.

Put the thinly pared rind of an orange or a lemon, a clove or two and a small piece of cinnamon stick into a half-bottle of the cheapest French grape brandy. Keep it at least a month before using it for puddings and cakes. It makes a delicious syllabub, and a refreshing drink topped up with soda water.

✣ *Culinary Hints* ✣

Water long boiled
Is tea spoiled.

And always warm the pot first.

To boil a cracked egg safely, add a generous spoonful of salt to the water before putting in the egg, or put in the egg and a pin together. To stop an egg cracking, pierce the pointed end with a pin before putting it in the pan.

When cooking pasta, a spoonful of cooking oil added to the water will not only prevent the pasta from sticking to the bottom of the pan and to itself, but will help stop the water boiling over too.

To help jellies set more quickly, stand the mould in a basin of cold water to which a handful of cooking salt has been added.

Both sorrel and lady's bedstraw (*Galium verum*) can be used instead of rennet to 'turn' milk for junket and cheese-making. Infuse a handful of either in the warm milk for about 10 minutes, then strain and leave to set.

If you have to make sandwiches from very fresh bread, try dipping the breadknife into boiling water before cutting each slice.

It isn't necessary to make *croûtons* for a soup or stew at the last minute; they can even be made the day before, provided they have been fried in plenty of really hot oil and well drained on kitchen paper. If you want to keep them warm, leave the oven door ajar so that they stay crisp. Keep them in an air-tight box.

For really crisp fried bread, dip each side of the bread *very briefly* in cold water before frying. Toasted bread is delicious fried.

Instant White Sauce

Measure the cold liquid, butter and flour into a saucepan and set it over a medium heat, whisking frequently with a wire whisk as the butter melts. Once the butter has melted, whisk continually until the mixture reaches boiling point and

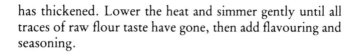

has thickened. Lower the heat and simmer gently until all traces of raw flour taste have gone, then add flavouring and seasoning.

Sauce Table

Thin	1 oz each butter and flour to 1 pint liquid
Medium	2 oz each butter and flour to 1 pint liquid
Thick	3 oz each butter and flour to 1 pint liquid

Mock Cream

Here is a very good mock cream, which fooled me when given to me by a Staffordshire friend. It is not particularly economical but at least it tastes good, which is more than can be said for many such recipes.

½ lb unsalted butter
½ pint milk
1 teaspoon powdered gelatine

Put the milk and butter in a pan and bring to boiling point. When the butter has melted, take the pan off the heat and add the gelatine. Stir constantly for about 2 minutes, cool the mixture to lukewarm, and then put it in the blender and blend until thick.

Children clamouring for sweets can be quietened by giving them a mixture of brown sugar and oatmeal in a twist of paper. This is an old country sweet, cheap and nourishing, with a lovely, nutty flavour.

Snow Pancakes

This recipe was given to me by a Cumbrian who told me that these pancakes were always made when a fall of snow had been made powdery by a hard frost. Damp snow will not do at all.

Make your usual pancake batter, and, just as you are ready to make the pancakes, whisk in to the batter a handful of frozen snow. The pancakes will be particularly light and crisp.

❧ *General Hints* ☙

To lengthen the life of ovenproof china, before using it for the first time, heat the china slowly in the oven and let it cool equally slowly, without taking it out of the switched-off oven.

Prepare new cast iron pans by heating vegetable oil in them to a deep-frying temperature; pour off the oil and rub the pan with kitchen salt and a paper towel.

Rub new baking tins with oil, heat them thoroughly in a hot oven and then wipe off the oil with paper towels. Wash all baking tins immediately after use, then put them to dry in the oven as it cools down.

Vegetables soon sour and corrode metals and glazed red ware, by which a strong poison is produced. Vinegar, by its acidity, does the same, the glazing being of lead or arsenic.

A New System of Domestic Cookery, 1818

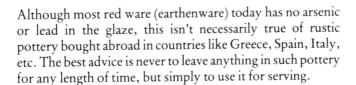

Although most red ware (earthenware) today has no arsenic or lead in the glaze, this isn't necessarily true of rustic pottery bought abroad in countries like Greece, Spain, Italy, etc. The best advice is never to leave anything in such pottery for any length of time, but simply to use it for serving.

Rhubarb leaves and apple or potato peelings are all useful in cleaning burnt saucepans. Boil up a handful of one of these in the pan to be treated, then leave the whole panful to stand overnight; the burnt bits should be very easy to clean the next morning. This treatment is *not* recommended for enamel pans.

Fish or onion smelling frying-pans are best washed up in cold water with a generous pinch of soda added, to get rid of the smell. If the pan is still greasy, wash again with plenty of washing-up liquid, but still using cold water.

Use cold water to scrub oniony chopping-boards too; hot water opens the grain of the wood and allows the smell to sink in.

Before boiling milk, rinse the pan out with cold water; the milk will not stick to the pan as much.

If the milk boils over on to a solid hotplate, sprinkle it with salt at once to stop the smell.

A large vase of marigolds on the kitchen table is supposed to absorb cooking smells and stop them permeating through the house. I don't really know how effective this is, but they look very pretty.

Southernwood, tansy, feverfew and lavender will all keep flies out of the kitchen and larder.

❧ *Household Work* ❧

Housework is undoubtedly a chore, and although there are some who enjoy it and others who loathe it, the feeling of satisfaction when the vacuum-cleaner is put away and the dusters rinsed out, the house now gleaming and tidy, is universally pleasurable. The word 'housework' represents a narrower area now than it did even 50 years ago, when there was still perhaps a small staff who could lift the cleaning tasks from the shoulders of the lady of the house and leave her free to do the no less important but more ladylike work of arranging the flowers, making pot-pourri and dusting the valuable porcelain. Now that all this has to be done by one, pot-plants have replaced cut flowers, pot-pourri is bought, rarely made, and the porcelain sold or shut away.

A great deal of the zeal which was used to achieve the perfect house must have been misdirected. A Cumbrian friend can remember her mother black-leading the grate, polishing its brass and then whitening even that bit of the hearth which lay directly underneath the coals. This was regularly done, every morning, the fire lit, and within ten minutes of its whitening, the hearth would be covered in ash. There was still time, however, to bake all the family supply of bread, brew gallons of wine (I still have the straw-covered stoneware demijohn in which she made toast wine), and make hooky rugs to cover the shining flags. Another woman I met recalled that the flags in the Yorkshire farm-house where she was brought up were kept permanently polished by the friction of sweeping up the sand sprinkled on the floor to absorb the wet and mud brought in on boots from the farmyard. The sand was always freshly applied in elaborate patterns, after the dirty sand had been swept up, to put a finishing touch to the spotless kitchen. These touches did make a house into a home, but the homes of the house-proud are often oppressive places. I have little sympathy for those who grumble about the mess that Christmas trees or catkins make. Doesn't the pleasure gained from these things more than compensate for the little extra vacuuming or dusting that has to be done?

A neighbour of ours, in his seventies and on his own, cleans his cottage from top to bottom every Friday morning without fail. If you are ever in doubt about what day of the week it is, a walk past his house, with the windows open and the noise of the vacuum drifting through them, and his dog sitting mournfully on the doorstep, will remind you. My own method is shamefully slapdash in the face of this masculine efficiency; I rarely give the house more than 'a lick and a promise' if people are coming to dinner, relying on the soft lights not to show up the cobwebs and the dog- and cat-hairs on the carpets. If friends are coming for the weekend, however, the whole cottage is scoured from top to bottom, as the merciless daylight will reveal every dusty surface and crumby corner.

46

All over the North of England particular care is taken to brighten the otherwise somewhat dour towns and terraces. Yellow donkey-stone is used to clean the flags in backyards in Cheshire, and north of Manchester lines of whitening are still drawn round the doorsteps 'to keep the devil away', and thwart the enveloping industrial dust which blackens everything else. (Now that whitening is becoming so hard to buy, white paint is used instead, and makes the task a monthly, rather than a daily, one.) The grimmer the area, the more valiant the effort made to extend painstaking household work to the outside of the house as well, for the benefit of the passer-by, and the self-esteem of the housewife herself.

❧ *Furniture* ☙

To clean old oak

Sponge the wood with warm beer to remove any grease. Boil 2 pints stale beer with ½ oz beeswax and ½ oz brown sugar until the sugar has dissolved and the wax melted. When cool, apply this mixture to the wood with a large soft brush, allow to dry, then rub hard to a high polish.

Furniture Polish

2 oz grated beeswax	1 oz soap flakes
1 pint boiling water	½ pint turpentine

Dissolve the soap and beeswax in the boiling water and stir as it cools. When lukewarm, add the turpentine and stir well.

Holme St Cuthbert Womens' Institute

Furniture Cream
Melt 3 oz white wax, add 8 oz turpentine (*not* over direct heat, as it is highly inflammable), then 8 fl oz warm water. Add enough ammonia, when the mixture is cool, to thicken it to a cream.

Beeswax and Turpentine Polish for Old Wood
Shred a block of beeswax into a pan and cover it with turpentine, then leave it in a warm place until the wax has dissolved. Stir very thoroughly, adding more turpentine if the mixture is too thick, or the polish will be sticky.

A Seventeenth-Century Polish
Melt beeswax and infuse crushed sweet cicely seeds in it for several days. Strain out the seeds and allow the wax to harden. Using this involves a great deal of rubbing as the polish is sticky, but the smell is lovely.

Liquid Polish for any surface
½ pint turpentine   ½ pint linseed oil
¼ pint methylated spirits   ¼ pint vinegar

Bottle and shake well before each using. This is very good for dark wood, and constant use helps prevent wood worm.

Leather Upholstery Polish
Mix ¼ pint vinegar with ½ pint linseed oil. Use this sparingly and polish immediately with a soft cloth.

To remove stains from table tops, rub with a mixture of equal parts of vegetable oil and methylated spirits.

To removing dents in furniture, fold a large sheet of brown paper into a pad and soak it in water. Hold this over the dented part and iron until all the moisture has dried out of the paper. Repeat if necessary, then polish.

To hide scratches on furniture, rub the scratch with half a freshly-cut brazil nut.

Clean plush, velvet or corduroy upholstery by dusting it with a clean chamois leather wrung out in cold water.

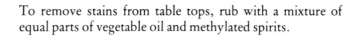 Floors

Scrubbing Mixture for flags, or untreated wood

1 lb soft soap	1 lb silver sand
1 lb coarse whitening	4 pints water

Put all the ingredients into a large pan and stir until it boils. Allow to simmer, stirring occasionally, until creamy, then cool and pour into old jam jars.

Scrubbing Mixture for Wood Floors

To clean neglected wood floors, boil 1 lb soft soap mixed with 1 lb Fuller's earth and 4 pints of water until this is reduced by half, and scrub the floor with it.

If grease is spilt on an unsealed wood floor, pour cold water on it at once to harden the grease and prevent it soaking in to the wood, then scrub it with the above cleaner.

Economical Floor Polish

8 oz wax candle ends
8 oz shredded soap (or soap flakes)
1 tablespoon linseed oil
1 tablespoon turpentine

Melt the candle ends and the soap in ¼ pint of boiling water, mixing well. When cool, add the linseed oil and the turpentine. Shake well, keep covered and use on wooden or unsealed cork floors.

Add a few drops of paraffin to the washing water when cleaning lino or tiles to give a gloss.

Lino Polish

1 cup paraffin
1 pint warm water
2 tablespoons milk

Put all the ingredients into a bottle and shake well. This polish is also good for paintwork.

To stain floors, clean them with the Scrubbing Mixture (see page 50), then dissolve 2 oz permanganate of potash in 1 pint boiling water and, wearing rubber gloves, brush this evenly on to the floor, following the grain of the wood. When dry, add further coats until the required depth of colour is reached. Leave for 24 hours, then polish well.

Flagged kitchen floors were often kept sprinkled with sand, a very practical idea when muddy boots tramped in and out. The sand absorbed the damp and made sweeping up much easier, while the friction helped to polish the flags at the same time. A conscientious housekeeper would sprinkle the sand in elaborate patterns, to put a finishing touch to her work.

⋙ Carpets and Rugs ⋘

Carpet Shampoo

Mix a little low-lather detergent with ½ pint boiling water. Add 1 teaspoon ammonia and a small lump of soda and mix well. Dip a brush in this, shake off the surplus and scrub the carpet, always in the same direction. Rinse with a cloth wrung out in warm water, and finally rub with a dry cloth.

To remove soot from a carpet, sprinkle it generously with salt and vacuum up quickly.

To remove candle-wax from carpets, remove as much of the hardened wax as possible with a blunt knife or spoon handle. Cover with several layers of brown or blotting paper and press with a hot iron so that the paper absorbs the melted wax. Finish with a few drops of lighter fuel on a clean cloth to remove the last traces of grease.

To remove oil, make a paste of Fuller's earth and boiling water, brush it over the stain and leave 24 hours before brushing off. Again, finish with a rag dipped in lighter fuel if necessary.

In most old books of household management one comes across directions for spreading damp tealeaves on the carpets, then brushing them off, to remove dust and dirt. In these days of vacuum cleaners this messy method is not strictly necessary, but it remains a good way of cleaning fragile and valuable carpets which should not be vacuumed. Save tea-leaves (or coffee-grounds) until you have enough to treat the rug in mind then, choosing a fine day so that you can do the job outside, spread the carpet out and sprinkle the tealeaves along one long edge, keeping back enough to put along one short edge afterwards. Brush the leaves across the carpet and right off the other side, then repeat with the rest of the leaves from top to bottom. Shake the rug well before taking it inside.

Persian and Turkish rugs can also be washed in the bath, in cold water. Leave the plug out of the plug-hole, put the rug in the bath and turn the cold tap full on, so that the rush of water drives out the dirt. Hang outside to dry, if possible, but not in full sunshine. A friend in Cumbria washes her carpets in a fast-flowing beck, where the soft water is particularly good for such carpets. An old method was to drag the rug, face down, over a dew-soaked lawn, but don't attempt this if the grass has recently been mown.

To wash sheepskin rugs, choose a dry, windy day. Make a lukewarm soapy solution in the bath, adding a little ammonia. Immerse the rug, and with bare feet get in with it and walk all over it to release the dirt. Pull the rug up to one end, pull out the plug and when all the dirty water has run out, refill the bath with cold water. Rinse at least 3 times, adding a little vinegar to the final rinse to help get rid of the soap. If you can hang the rug outside on a line and turn the hose on it, so much the better. Keep fluffing out the wool as the rug dries, and if the back shows signs of hardening, beat it hard with a broom handle or carpet beater to soften it. All this may sound laborious, but it is very expensive to have these rugs cleaned, and this method works perfectly well.

To stop rugs curling up at the edges, sew boned petersham (like that used for waistbands) along each edge, keeping the edge of the petersham flush with the edge of the rug.

To Make a Hooky Rug
This tip was given to me by an old friend in Cumbria whose mother used to make all the kitchen rugs in this way, in

common with households all over England. She had a wooden frame, like a giant embroidery frame, to hold the sacking taut while she threaded the strips through. Old work clothes in dull blues, greys, blacks and browns formed the background, while any jollier rags, such as those from red flannel petticoats, formed the design. Cut old woollen rags into strips 1 in wide and 6 in long. Wash a hessian sack and spread it out flat to dry. Make two holes close together with a wooden skewer and poke a strip of cloth through to make a double tuft on the right side of the sack; continue like this until the whole of the sack is densely covered, working in the design as you go. If any patch looks a little bald, work in a few more strips (worn patches of the rug can be repaired in this way, too). Sew another sack over the back of the rug to make it extra hard-wearing.

Floor Covering for Bedrooms

Sew together the cheapest common cloth, the size of the room, and tack the edges to the floor. Now paper the cloth as you would the walls of a room, with cheap room paper; putting a border round the edge if desired. The paste will be the better if a little gum arabic is mixed with it. When thoroughly dry, give it two coats of furniture or carriage varnish.

Dr Chase's Receipts, 1880

This American tip may sound curious but can look extremely attractive. If the floor has a good flat surface, wallpaper can be stuck over it (use a rubber-based glue which can be removed if you tire of the paper on the floor), and varnished with two coats of polyurethane varnish. I have treated two bathroom floors in this way, both covered with worn lino; one I treated with an ordinary but very pretty wrapping paper, the other with a collage of garden pages cut from glossy magazines. Both needed no upkeep other than the re-application of varnish every other year, but this would depend on the amount of traffic the floor received.

❧ *Cleaning Metals* ☙

Scouring Powder for pans

Shake together 1 lb whitening, 1 lb pumice powder and 1 lb soap powder, and keep in screw-top jars.

Clean neglected pewter by mixing scouring powder with a little methylated spirits and giving a final polish with paraffin.

Early engravers used to use crushed mares' tail (*Hippuris vulgaris*) to clean their engraving plates. It can be used for cleaning brass, copper and pewter, a tip worth knowing if you are plagued with it in the garden.

To clean blackened brass, mix 2 parts flour and one part salt to a paste with vinegar. Leave this on the brass to dry, wash off and polish. A final rub with a chamois gives a good shine. This is a good tip for cleaning copper too.

To clean silver and plate, dissolve ½ oz each of cream of tartar, common salt and alum in 4 pints of water. Wash the silver in this, rinse and polish.

Silver-polishing Cloth

Dissolve 4 oz soap flakes in ¼ pint of boiling water. Add 2 oz whitening and 1 tablespoon ammonia and beat until the mixture becomes a jelly. Soak a duster in this overnight, next day wring it out and leave to dry.

To remove light rusting from iron and steel (this does not work if the rust has already eaten into the metal). Using finest emery paper damped with paraffin, rub in one direction only to avoid a scratched look. For steel, wood-ash can replace the emery paper with advantage; dip a rag in paraffin first, then in the ash.

To prevent iron and steel rusting in storage, melt 2 oz wax with 1 oz rosin, strain while still hot and apply a light coat.

To polish iron and steel fenders, rub them with warm mutton fat and buff them with unslaked lime.

❧ Fires ☙

To make coal burn longer, dissolve a large handful of washing soda in half a bucket of warm water and throw it over about a hundredweight of coal. Allow it to dry out. This is supposed to improve the burning power by 25 per cent.

Coal dust is invaluable for keeping up a good fire; use it damped with a little water when banking up a fire for the night.

Small coal wetted makes the strongest fire for the back, but must remain untouched until it cake.

A New System of Domestic Cookery, 1818

Clay-balls for fires. Shape damp clay into egg-sized balls and allow to dry thoroughly in a warm, dry place. Add 6–10 to an ordinary coal fire. They radiate heat well and do not disintegrate for some time.

When clearing out a fire, keep the largest cinders to start the next fire, and for 'backing'.

Collect fir-cones whenever possible to use as firelighters, and save orange and lemon peel for the same purpose. They all contain quantities of natural oils which will start a fire off well.

Burn a tin can on the fire to help eliminate the soot in the chimney. All the people who gave me this tip swore by it, and a scientist friend explained that the metal oxides given off by the burning tin might help to catalyse the combustion of soot in the chimney. Add the tin when the fire has got going properly and leave it there for as long as the fire is alight. It quickly becomes black and looks undistinguishable from coal or logs. Use a fresh tin for each new fire.

Chimneys belonging to wood-burning fires and stoves are particularly difficult to sweep, because the soot is so sticky. One tip is to stand on the roof and let down your old Christmas tree on a rope, having remembered to tack a damp blanket across the hearth first, if it is an open one. Apart from the obvious hazards and difficulties involved in getting a fir tree up on a roof, this is supposed to be a very effective method.

A traditional rhyme giving the burning qualities of each type of wood, worth learning if you can choose your wood:

> Beechwood fires burn bright and clear,
> Hornbeam blazes too,
> Keep the logs above a year
> They'll be seasoned through.
> Pine is good, so is yew,
> For warmth thro' wintry days.
> The poplar and the willow too
> Take long to make a blaze.
> Oaken logs will warm you well
> If they are good and dry.
> Larch will of the pinewoods smell
> And the sparks will fly.

Birchen logs will burn so fast,
Alder not at all.
Chestnut logs full long will last
If cut and let to fall.
Logs of pear and apple logs,
Bring scent into the room.
Cherry logs laid on the dogs
Smell like flowers in bloom,
But ashen logs, so smooth and grey,
You burn them green or old,
Cut them, all you can each day,
They're worth their weight in gold.

🌿 *General hints* 🌿

To clean Looking-glasses. Remove the fly-stains, and other
soil, by a damp rag; then polish with woollen rag and
powder blue.

A New System of Domestic Cookery, 1818

To prevent the creaking of a Door. Rub a bit of soap on the
hinges.

A New System of Domestic Cookery, 1818

To destroy Crickets. Put Scotch snuff upon the holes where
they come out.

A New System of Domestic Cookery, 1818

Freshen sick-rooms by having a bunch of fresh feverfew (*tanacetum parthenium*) and southernwood (*Artemisia abrotanum*) in a jug on a table by the patient; both herbs are powerful disinfectants. Other methods were to set light to a spoonful of eau de cologne and carry it round the room, to burn juniper berries or an apple stuck with cloves (as in Mrs Gaskell's *Cranford*), or a lump of camphor in a saucer of coffee-grounds, feeding the burning camphor with the grounds. Another idea was to hang a peeled onion in the room, as it was supposed to absorb the germs and prevent infection spreading from patient to nurse — it can't have done much to freshen the atmosphere.

To take stains out of Marble. Mix unslaked lime, in finest powder, with the strongest soap-lye, pretty thick; and instantly with a painter's brush, lay it on the whole of the marble. In two months time wash it off perfectly clean, then have ready a fine thick lather of soft soap, boiled in soft water, dip a brush in it, and scour the marble with powder, this will, by a very good rubbing, give a beautiful polish. Clear off the soap and finish with a smooth hard brush till the end be effected.

A New System of Domestic Cookery, 1818

For removing cigarette burns from marble, use a cream bath cleaner, and give a final polish with milk.

If a ground-glass stopper has become jammed in the neck of a bottle or decanter, try dropping a little cooking oil round the neck with a feather, and standing the bottle in a warm place for an hour or so. Hit the stopper gently with the handle of a wooden spoon to loosen it, and it should come out quite easily.

To clean decanters

There are several remedies for removing the deposit from the bottoms of decanters and water bottles, all equally effective. All involve adding the substance to water in the decanter and swirling it around until the deposit is removed: crushed egg-shell (my preferred method), grated raw potato and a little vinegar, lead shot, sand (effective but not always easy to rinse out), mustard-seed (which absorbs any stale smell as well). Never use detergent of any sort.

Drying a decanter is not easy, but this method gets rid of almost all the water. Fill the decanter to the brim with cold water, turn it quickly upside down and allow it to empty while the cold tap runs at full force over the upturned base. This miraculously disposes of all but a drop or two of water. Allow the decanter to dry out in a dry room before replacing the stopper.

Store wine glasses either in the open air, or, if in a cupboard, upside down. This is to avoid any mustiness which has collected in the glass spoiling the flavour of wine drunk from them.

Stack fine china with tissue paper between each item, to prevent the glaze being scratched. Even modern, dishwasher-proof china needs this treatment.

How to lay a table for a dinner party (1926, but still useful):

Put the glasses on the right, next to the soup-spoon, placing the tallest glass furthest from the diner to prevent it being knocked over. Lay cutlery by starting from the outside and working in — soup-spoon first, then the knife for the fish course, knife for the main course, etc. with corresponding forks on the left. Place the dessert knife with the blade pointing to the left above the table-mat, the dessert spoon, also pointing left, comes beneath that, then the dessert fork under that, pointing right. Place finger-bowls at the top left corner.

Clean the blades of carbon steel knives with a cork dipped in scouring powder, rinse well, then polish to a soft shine with a cotton cloth. Before putting the knives away, rub each blade over with a paper towel and a little cooking oil to prevent rusting.

The smell of onions can be removed from knife blades by pushing them once or twice into clean earth, then washing in cold water.

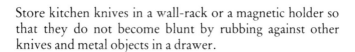

Store kitchen knives in a wall-rack or a magnetic holder so that they do not become blunt by rubbing against other knives and metal objects in a drawer.

Remove egg stains from silver spoons by rubbing with salt before washing them up.

Salt will remove the burn marks from the edges of pie dishes; salt and vinegar will also remove the stains from inside flower vases.

A tablespoon of vinegar in the washing-up water helps to remove grease; gilt mirror and picture frames can be washed with a weak mixture of vinegar and water, and furniture rubbed with diluted vinegar before polishing has a brighter shine.

To clean ivory, pick a sunny day, then wash the ivory in a lukewarm soapy lather, cleaning any carving with an old toothbrush. Stand it in the bright sunshine for several hours to 'bleach' the ivory, at the same time keeping it damp so that it won't warp. Dry well. If the ivory is stained, remove the stains, if possible, with precipitated chalk mixed with lemon juice, during the initial washing.

63

To clean and repair tortoiseshell, clean it with manicure cream or almond oil and polish with a chamois leather. To mend it, tie or bind the broken edges together with cotton tape (*not* sticky tape), heat a metal skewer until very hot and press the broken parts with it until they fuse.

Remove hot water scorch marks from japanned trays by rubbing with vegetable oil until the marks disappear; polish with dry flour and a soft cloth.

Fountain pens can be cleaned by soaking all the parts in vinegar for half-an-hour, then rinsing and drying thoroughly. The vinegar effectively dissolves any dried ink sediment.

Hardened paintbrushes can be cleaned by boiling them in vinegar for 15 minutes. Stand the brushes upright in a saucepan and pour in vinegar to come 7/8ths of the way up the bristles, avoiding the part where the bristles are glued into the handle. Simmer for quarter of an hour, rinse well and dry in a draught. A strong solution of Jeyes Fluid will also clean paintbrushes; leave them in it overnight.

Wicker baskets last longer if scrubbed every so often with soapy water and salt. Dry out of doors.

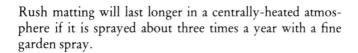

Rush matting will last longer in a centrally-heated atmosphere if it is sprayed about three times a year with a fine garden spray.

Sagging cane and wicker chair seats can be revived by covering them with a damp cloth for an hour or so. This treatment also helps to prolong the life of cane chairs if you have central heating, as cane and wicker become very brittle if allowed to get too dry.

Wicker chairs can be washed with soapy water containing a little salt; use as little water as possible, rinse with cold water to harden the wicker, and include some lemon juice in the final rinse to whiten. Dry out of doors, or in a draught, but not by direct heat (you can use a hair-dryer, on a low setting, if you must hasten the process). If the wicker is dark brown, don't wash it at all, just brush it all over to get rid of the dust, then rub with a little paraffin, drying it outside to get rid of the smell.

Wash coconut fibre doormats with hot water and soda, rinse well with a hose or watering-can, then give a final brush with salt and water to stiffen the fibres.

Natural sponges can be washed by working a solution of 1 teaspoon permanganate of potash in 2 pints of warm water through them for about 10 minutes. Rinse thoroughly.

Hair-brushes and combs should be washed in warm water and a little ammonia. The brushes can be given a second wash in washing-up liquid and warm water; rinse well and dry away from direct heat.

Clean chamois leathers by kneading them in warm soapy water and ammonia; do not rub them. Rinse well, squeeze gently and pull and stretch the leathers while they dry to keep them supple.

To revive the bounce in old tennis balls, warm them gently in a low oven overnight. This also revives flagging batteries, and my daughter's method with the latter is to stick them to her bedroom radiator overnight with blue-tack, which she swears works very efficiently, but won't do anything for dead batteries.

To help keep damp cellars and larders dry, stand 8 oz jars of salt (or lime) in each corner. Both salt and lime can be dried out and re-used.

To keep dustbins clean and sweet with the minimum of fuss, simply burn a couple of newspapers in them after they have been emptied, every week in the summer. This is not, needless to say, a good idea if your local council has just gone over to plastic bins, as ours has.

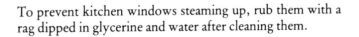

To prevent kitchen windows steaming up, rub them with a rag dipped in glycerine and water after cleaning them.

All glass responds very well to being polished with damp newspaper; it is the printers' ink which gives the shine.

When replacing a pane of glass, once the broken glass has been taken out, remove the old putty by rubbing it with a red hot poker or soldering iron.

When hammering nails into very hard wood, grease them lightly first and they will go in far more easily. Old carpenters used to rub the nail alongside their noses, to give just the right amount of grease.

To support brooms and mops, put two large nails or screws in the wall about 1½ to 2 in apart. Drop the broom down between them, head up.

Remove paint splashes and new putty from windows with hot vinegar.

To paper a damp room. Take ½ pint alum and ½ lb glue size, dissolve together in a pan of boiling water. Take off old paper and wash wall twice with the above solution. Re-paper when dry.

A Women's Institute tip

Always keep some spare wallpaper when first hanging it, and leave a piece to fade in the sun so that, if you need to repair a faded patch of paper, you have faded paper with which to do it. When repairing a small area, tear the paper rather than cutting it, so that the edges blend better.

Stand a pail of cold water containing a handful of hay in a newly-painted room to absorb the smell. A peeled onion performs the same task, but not as pleasantly.

Try not to hang pictures on a damp wall, as this will cause 'foxing' to the mount. Mounts can be cleaned with stale bread, changing each piece as it becomes dirty. This is more effective than using a pencil rubber, as the surface of the mount itself is not worn away.

An Edwardian tip for hanging pictures suggests sticking a slice of cork in each corner at the back, so that there is a gap between wall and picture for ventilation, and to prevent marking the wall.

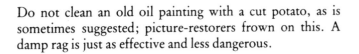

Do not clean an old oil painting with a cut potato, as is sometimes suggested; picture-restorers frown on this. A damp rag is just as effective and less dangerous.

When leaving a house empty in the winter, apart from doing the obvious things like checking the lagging round pipes and tanks, put a tablespoon of salt in lavatory cisterns and bowls to prevent the water freezing, and put plugs in baths, sinks and basins (but do not press them in too firmly). To be really safe, turn off the water at the mains and drain down the system by running all the taps, but make sure you have turned off all water heating appliances first.

When leaving a house empty at any time, pull all plugs out of their sockets (except where the appliance must remain on), particularly if you are in any doubt about your electric wiring. And shut the doors to all the rooms, to help stop any fire spreading.

To keep a supply of matches dry in damp conditions, dip the head of each one in a saucepan of melted candle-wax and let it harden before returning it to its box. This may sound laborious, but not all of us carry lighters, and camping holidays can be very wet. The matches do flare up more than usual when you strike them, so let children handle them with extra care.

Flowers, Fresh and Dried, for the House

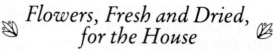

The following is a reasonably comprehensive list of how to make most herbaceous flowers last longer in water. I found it laboriously written out in the back of a book called *The Woman's Treasury for Home and Garden*, bought at a jumble sale. This list was far more useful than anything that the book itself contained, and I am very grateful to its unknown author.

How to make cut flowers last

Flower	Preparation	Add to vase
Anemone	Cut stems on slant, submerge to heads 1–2 hours until texture of flowers is firm	¼ cup vinegar to 2 cups water
Asters	Place stems in boiling water 1 minute	2 tablespoons sugar to 1 quart water
Begonias	Pick and arrange as quickly as possible	1 tablespoon salt to 1 quart water
Carnations	Pick fully open, cut stems on slant between notches	Cold water only
Chrysanths	Crush stems, hold in boiling water 2–3 mins then in cold	5 drops oil cloves to 1 quart water
Cosmos	Pick when centre is smooth before pollen ripens	1 teaspoon sugar to 1 quart water
Daffodils	Cut above white stem base, place in 1 in very cold water and leave in cool place half an hour	1–2 in water only
Dahlias	Place in 2–3 in boiling water 1 minute then in cold. Change water daily	5 tablespoons medical alcohol to 2 quarts water
Delphiniums	Cut stems under water, place in boiling water 1 minute then in cold	2 teaspoons sugar to 1 pint water
Gaillardias	Stems in boiling water for 1 minute	2 tablespoons salt to 1 pint water
Gladioli	Pick when first florets are open	5 tablespoons vinegar to 1 quart water
Grasses	Dip stems in vinegar	Cold water only

Flower	Preparation	Add to vase
Hydrangea	Pick well-developed, firm heads, remove most leaves, crush stem, boiling water 1 minute	Cold water only
Iris	Pick when just opening, cut above white stem under water, dip in boiling water 1 minute, place in deep water	3 drops peppermint oil to 1 quart water
Larkspur	Pick when first flowers are open, place in boiling water 1 minute	Cold water only
Leaves, Beech, etc	Submerge in water overnight	Preserve in 1 part glycerine 2 parts water for 3 weeks
Evergreen leaves	As above	1 tablespoon glycerine to 1 quart water
Marguerites	Pick before pollen ripens	1 tablespoon salt to 1 quart water
Marigolds	Place in boiling water 1 minute	1 tablespoon sugar to 1 pint water
Peonies	Place in boiling water 30 seconds only	3 tablespoons sugar to 1 quart water
Poppies	Pick when bud is upright, or at sunrise when just opening. Boil ends 1 minute, plunge in deep water	Cold water only
Primroses	Dip stems in boiling water 30 seconds only	Cold water only
Roses	Cut stem diagonally or scrape ½ in stem, dip in boiling water 1–2 minutes, arrange in warm water	2 tablespoons salt to 1 quart water. If silver vase, add 2 copper coins
Scabious	Pick when 1 circle of flowers or petals is open	Cold water only
Schizanthus	Pick when about 8 flowers are open	Cold water only
Snapdragon	Cut stems diagonally with sharp knife. Never store with other flowers as they give off a gas which kills other blooms	1 tablespoon salt to 1 quart warm water
Spirea	Shake to dislodge loose petals. Smash stem ends with a hammer	Cold water only
Statice	Pick when fully open	3 tablespoons sugar to 1 quart water
Stocks	Remove most foliage, crush stems, then dip in boiling water 2–3 minutes	1 tablespoon salt to 1 pint water

71

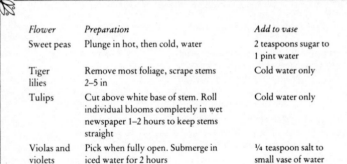

Flower	Preparation	Add to vase
Sweet peas	Plunge in hot, then cold, water	2 teaspoons sugar to 1 pint water
Tiger lilies	Remove most foliage, scrape stems 2–5 in	Cold water only
Tulips	Cut above white base of stem. Roll individual blooms completely in wet newspaper 1–2 hours to keep stems straight	Cold water only
Violas and violets	Pick when fully open. Submerge in iced water for 2 hours	¼ teaspoon salt to small vase of water

If you are using crumpled wire to arrange flowers, use a pinch of borax in the water to prevent it rusting.

Crush the stems of any woody plants or shrubs before arranging them. Remove most of the leaves for lilac and philadelphus.

Add a copper coin to the water for any flowers with sticky sap, such as daffodils, narcissi, hyacinths, etc.

To help berries last longer, put a dessertspoon of glycerine into a pint of water and bring to the boil. Stand the stems in a metal container and pour the boiling mixture over stems to a depth of 2–3 inches. Leave for 24 hours, then arrange in fresh water. This does not preserve the berries, it simply extends their life.

Infuse foxglove leaves in hot water. Cool, strain and use about ¼ pint in the vase to prolong the life of other cut flowers. As the drug digitalis is obtained from foxgloves, do not leave this infusion sitting about to be drunk by the unwary.

To dry flowers, pick them on a dry day, following the directions in the preceding table for the best time for each type of flower. Hang them upside down in bunches in a dry airy place until fully dry; if they are arranged too soon, the heads will droop.

Beech, oak and hawthorn leaves, and ferns, can be pressed dry, thus keeping them green. Simply arrange them carefully between plenty of newspaper and put them under the carpet. Leave them for about 2 months, then arrange.

For dried arrangements mix 2 tablespoons water with 1 heaped cup of detergent.

Leeks, onions and best of all, artichokes (globe), produce lovely flowers which dry very well.

Herb Sachets
Lavender is the most common and still perhaps the nicest; cut the lavender on a dry day and hang it to dry in the airing

73

cupboard until the flowers can be easily rubbed from the stalks. Make up small sachets in pretty cotton fabrics, fill them with lavender and tie each tightly at the neck with ribbon (preferably not nylon, as this may slip undone and the sachet discard lots of grey lavender everywhere). Sweet geranium leaves, lemon balm, eau de cologne mint and woodruff all make good sachets.

The yearly harvesting of lavender helps keep this otherwise leggy plant in good shape.

❧ *Pot-Pourri* ☙

Pick rose petals on a dry day from fully open but not overblown roses. Spread on newspaper and dry on a sunny windowsill or in the airing cupboard. Dry other scented petals in the same way, preparing each in its season and storing in paper bags until all are ready: pinks, violets, wallflowers, lavender, mignonette, woodruff, etc. Add balm leaves, scented geranium, thyme and sweetbriar, bay and myrtle leaves. Mix with dried grated orange and lemon rind. Add kitchen salt, sea salt, a little brown sugar, gum benjamin and powdered orris root. Mix thoroughly, sprinkle with a little vinegar, put into a jar and stir every day. Keep the jar covered, only removing the lid when you want to scent the room, so that the pot-pourri will last longer. Amounts need not be very exact.

'Bay salt' is often mentioned in old pot-pourri recipes, but as this was only a type of sea salt, use that instead, or

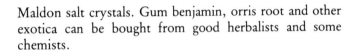

Maldon salt crystals. Gum benjamin, orris root and other exotica can be bought from good herbalists and some chemists.

Another pot-pourri recipe

Take any scented rose petals, prepared as above. Sprinkle salt on them and leave for a week, then add 40 drops oil of lavender, 4 oz powdered orris root, 20 drops oil of cloves, 10 drops oil of cinnamon and 6 oz angelica root.

A quicker Sort of Sweet Pot

Take three handfuls of orange-flowers, three of clove-gillyflowers, three of damask roses, one of knotted marjoram, one of lemon thyme, six bay leaves, a handful of rosemary, one of myrtle, half one of mint, one of lavender, the rind of a lemon, and a quarter of an ounce of cloves. Chop all and put them in layers, with pounded bay salt, between, up to the top of the jar. If all the ingredients cannot be got at once, put them in as you get them; always throwing in salt with every new article.

A New System of Domestic Cookery, 1818

A winter Pot-Pourri

Save lemon, orange and tangerine peel and pulverise it in the blender. Mix it with salt, broken pieces of cinnamon stick, freshly grated nutmeg, roughly crushed cloves, allspice and juniper berries, then stir in a few drops of oil of cloves. Add a little powdered orris root as a fixative, and some dried sweet geranium leaves, as they are generally available through the winter.

Pomander Hedgehogs

A pomander hedgehog is useful to have as a standby to take as a present for a child ill in bed. Full directions for making pomander balls are given on page 91. To make a hedgehog, take a lemon and stick cloves all over it, but leave the pointed end bare, for the face, with two cloves for eyes. Leave the underside bare of cloves, too, so that the hedgehog will stay the right way up and not roll over. Dry for at least a week in a warm place.

Skeleton leaves can make very pretty Christmas cards, and although fiddly to make, the careful child will find it fun. Robust evergreen leaves are the best subjects, with holly the most obvious choice. Put the leaves in a saucepan with water to cover them by about 2 in, add a large tablespoonful of washing soda, bring the water to the boil and simmer for about 5 minutes, then put the lid on the pan, take it off the heat and leave it for about 2 hours. Drain the leaves and spread them out on a wooden board; brush each leaf firmly but gently with a medium-firm toothbrush to remove the substance of the leaf from the veins. Put the skeletonised leaves between two sheets of blotting paper and press them for at least 24 hours. They can then be sprayed with gold, silver or bronze paint, or bleached in a weak solution of peroxide.

Tangerine Lanterns

I saw directions for making these in a popular magazine which cheated by using a night-light. The whole fun and point of making these is that they are night-lights in their own right.

Roll the tangerine between the palms of the hands to loosen the skin, then draw a line with a sharp knife round the hemisphere of the fruit. Gently ease away the skin from the flesh with your thumbs, then take out the flesh segment by segment in order to leave the pith 'core' attached to one half of the skin — this is the wick. When the skin is in two halves, drip candle-wax round and over the wick (trimming it if it is too long). You can use lard, but it doesn't smell as nice. Cut a hole about the size of a 2p piece in the other half of the skin. Light the wick and put the lid on top. Your lantern should last for about 15 minutes at least, and as the top chars a little, the smell is wonderful. We were taught how to make these as children and I've never known a child who wasn't enchanted by these lanterns.

❧ *Wardrobe and Laundry* ☙

To explore the laundries of stately and even not-so-stately homes is to re-enter the nightmare world of the pre-washing machine era, with huge coppers, deep enough to swallow young laundry-maids, boiled quantities of heavy linen, which then had to be hauled out and fed into that terrifying machine, the box-mangle. This was a box filled with stones that pressed water out of wet cloth by passing over wooden rollers when a handle was turned, in itself a heavy task. The racks for drying the clothes indoors stood ten feet tall, so it can't have been an easy matter arranging enormous wet sheets on the top rungs, or even pegging them on lines in the drying-green on a blustery day. Once all was dry, the ironing began, with every conceivable shape of iron for every imaginable type of frill, pleat and ruffle, but at least there was space to accomplish these Herculean feats in the large houses; for the ordinary housewife it must have been very difficult. A fine day meant that the heavy sheets and work sheets flapped dry outside in a few hours, a wet one that the washing steamed and dripped in the low-ceilinged kitchen, sometimes taking two days to dry properly. Washing machines, tumble and spin dryers and non-iron fabrics have eliminated almost all the nightmares from wash-day, and the only good thing that can be said for the old methods was that they were put to good use in 'rehabilitating' young girls who had 'fallen from virtue'. The constant process of restoring dirty linen to its fomer pristine state was thought to have a cleansing psychological effect on both mind and soul.

If laundering has changed completely, so has the care of clothes in general, as it had to, when ladies' maids were no longer part of the average household's staff. Sewing buttons on is an infuriating job, but how much worse it must have been when there were so many more buttons — on chemises, vests, petticoats, rows of them down the front of bodices, rows of them up the sides of children's gaiters, and some which even had to be removed before washing a garment, and replaced afterwards. Mud had to be brushed from the hems of long skirts, and dust from the folds of heavy cloth dresses; beautiful lace was fragile and tore easily, which resulted in darning so fine that eyes were ruined by trying to work in poor light. Some fabrics were as punishing to wear as to maintain; I can remember the exquisite comfort of the first party-frock I had which wasn't made of scratchy organdie. Organdie was misery to wear — the puff sleeves rubbed my arms, the frilled skirt made sitting down very hard on the backs of the legs — and misery for my mother to iron. Then along came nylon, comfortable *and* pretty, and practical, so that I didn't have to worry about ice-cream down the front, or patches of mud on the skirt, as it could be washed and dripped-dry within an hour. Nylon was regarded as grand enough for the most formal 'evening gowns' (as they were called then), and my mother had one in the 1950s which looked as if it was made of silver birch bark. The hazards of these new easy-care fabrics became obvious when anyone tried ironing this new and untried material, and the bottom of the iron was coated with a melted mass. I cheerfully forgo the advantages of polyester and acrylic for the comfort of cotton and the warmth of wool, at least I have the luxury of choice, which those poor Victorian laundry-maids had not.

Very recently, a Gallup survey deemed us to be a dirty nation. The Association of British Launderers and Cleaners disclosed that more than half the population had taken nothing to the cleaners for the past three months. This, of course, reveals more about the enormously high cost of having cleaning done professionally and the increasing use of man-made washable fibres, than it does about our personal cleanliness. The tips in this chapter I hope will indicate that it is quite unnecessary to risk sending your precious clothes to the cleaners, or even, if you have easy-care bed linen, to risk sending your washing to the laundry.

❧ Dry Cleaning ☙

For home dry-cleaning, a sleeve-pressing board is a help, but not essential (it is also useful if you make your own clothes); an efficient iron, preferably steam, and a comfortable ironing board may seem obvious, but many of my friends have totally inadequate equipment, which drives them to brand ironing a bore (it is, but you may as well be comfortable). In addition you will need a bottle of ammonia and one of perchloroethylene, both available from chemists and hardware shops, and both poisonous, so they should be kept away from children. The latter may be had under various proprietory names, such as Dabitoff. Several clean rags, a clothes brush and a large roll of wide sticky tape are also helpful. It may also be worth while, if you are married to a suit-wearer, to buy a trouser-press — not necessarily electric — which usually has a properly shaped hanger for the jacket as well. This is an unattractive and bulky gadget, but it does help to keep garments in very good shape.

Spread the garment to be cleaned out on the ironing board and look first for any grease spots. Treat these one by one with the perchloroethylene, rubbing in widening circles round the stain so as not to leave a noticeable ring. Rub collars and cuffs with this too, to remove greasy dirt. Then make a solution of 1 teaspoon ammonia and ½ pint of warm water and, using the clothes brush, brush this over the garment, taking care not to saturate it, and paying particular attention to areas of greatest wear, the seat, knees and front of thighs for trousers, elbows and fronts of jackets, etc.

Hang the garment up for about 30 minutes, then press it carefully with a damp cloth and medium hot iron. Put trousers with the leg seams together and, taking particular care to see where the last crease went, press along that, or you will end up with 'tram-lines' (the indication of a poor valet).

Finally, remove any bits of fluff, etc. with sticky tape. This is by far the most effective clothes brush: simply hold a 6 in length stretched between your hands and rub in the direction of the fabric's pile, renewing the tape when it has lost its stickiness. Hang the garment up to air before putting it away.

Note: Both ammonia and cleaning fluids need to be used with good ventilation.

When cleaning and pressing pleated skirts, tack the pleats loosely in place round the hem first.

Pressing any hem can leave a clear ridge round the bottom of a garment. Eliminate this by either putting a folded teacloth against the top of the hem, so that there is no change of level for the iron to show up, or by simply pressing the hem fold, and not ironing over the hem edge at all. The first is the best method.

❧ *Stains on Non-washable Fabrics* ❧

Wine: Sprinkle salt on the stain immediately, then sponge out with cold water as soon as possible.

Grease: Sprinkle thickly with talcum powder (Italian restaurants often have a tin standing by to rescue the clothes of splashy pasta eaters). Brush off when dry and use a dry-cleaning fluid to remove the stain completely.

Other stains, such as fruit, grass, etc: Dissolve 1 tablespoon borax in 1 pint warm water and use this to sponge off the stain, which should be tackled as soon as possible.

Paint: If it is water-based, sponge it off with cold water before the paint sets into the fibres of the fabric. For all other oil-based paints, use turpentine while the paint is still fresh, then sponge with methylated spirits in warm water (about 1 teaspoon meths to 1 cup water). If either type of paint has set, scrape as much as possible off with a blunt knife before proceeding as above.

Tar: Scrape off the tar itself with a blunt knife, then work on the stain with dry-cleaning fluid.

Ball-point and felt-tip pens: Some felt-tip pen ink can be removed with water, but most will respond better to dry-cleaning fluid or lighter fuel.

❧ *Laundering* ❧

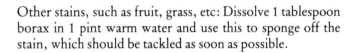

Washing Soap

1 lb caustic soda	2½ pints boiling water
6½ lb clarified fat	A few drops pine disinfectant

When making this recipe, wear rubber gloves and stand well back to avoid being splashed.

To clarify the fat, melt it and simmer for 10 minutes, then pour on a kettleful of boiling water. Stir, then allow to stand until cool, when the fat can be skimmed off. Mix the soda with 2½ pints boiling water. Stir in the fat gently until dissolved, and add the pine disinfectant. Pour into a shallow wooden box lined with a damp cloth and leave to stand until next day. Cut into blocks and leave to harden for about 6 weeks.

Soft Soap

1 lb potash
1 lb clarified fat
2 gallons water

Place the potash in a large pan with the water. Heat until the potash has dissolved, then add the fat and when all is well mixed, pour into a large stoneware jar. Stir thoroughly every day for a week, until it has become a jelly. It keeps well and can be used for all washing jobs.

Do use a low-foam detergent in your washing machine; very expensive repairs might be the result if you don't. Ordinary detergents producing too much foam mean that the foam can leak into the working parts of the machine.

Use a fabric conditioner in the final rinse for all man-made fibres such as nylon, terylene, polyester, acrylic, etc., even if you have soft water. It not only softens the fabrics, but

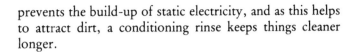

prevents the build-up of static electricity, and as this helps to attract dirt, a conditioning rinse keeps things cleaner longer.

To wash terylene net curtains with the very minimum of creasing, fold the curtains into a rectangle which will fit your sink or wash-basin and make a solution of warm water, low-foam detergent and 1 tablespoon ammonia. Soak the folded curtains in this, pressing to release the dirt. Rinse thoroughly, without unfolding them. Add a little sugar to the final rinse to act as a stiffener, if you like. Carry them to the line, unfold them and peg up to drip dry. They should need no ironing at all.

This is a much better method than washing them in the washing machine, when they usually end up creased even on a drip-dry cycle.

To wash fine silk, wash as for wool, spraying any dirty patches with one of the aerosol stain-removing sprays such as Frend or Shout first. Rinse thoroughly, adding a pinch of borax to the rinsing water to give lustre and body to the silk. Roll in a towel until ready to iron, then iron on the wrong side. Hang on a padded hanger to finish drying.

An Edwardian recipe for cleaning silk gauze
Mix 6 oz honey with 4 oz soft soap. Dilute with ½ pint gin. Brush the solution gently into the fabric with a soft brush.

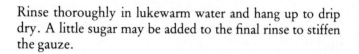

Rinse thoroughly in lukewarm water and hang up to drip dry. A little sugar may be added to the final rinse to stiffen the gauze.

Wash wool sweaters (unless machine washable) in *cold* water and Stergene, rinse thoroughly and finish with a fabric conditioner. Give a short spin, and iron while still slightly damp, on the wrong side, with a steam iron.

To wash eiderdowns, those filled with man-made fibres can be put in the washing-machine, on a drip-dry programme. Feather quilts can be washed in plenty of lukewarm soapy water in the bath, with the usual addition of a little ammonia. Rinse thoroughly, with a drop of ammonia in each rinsing water. They can then be given a short spin in the washing-machine or spin-dryer (I don't advise a tumble-dryer), or put once through a mangle. Hang up the eiderdown in the open air, taking it off the line at frequent intervals to give it a good shake to redistribute the feathers.

Removing stains from washable fabrics

Ball-point pen: Rub with methylated spirits.

Felt-tip pen: This can often be removed with water, so try this first, then use meths, as above.

Tea: Soak the stain in a strong solution of borax and water; a stale stain may take 1–2 days.

Coffee: Rub glycerine into the stain, then rinse in tepid water.

Cocoa: Rub stains at once with cold water and soap. If the stain is stale, proceed as for tea.

Fruit: While still fresh and damp cover with talcum powder, let it dry and brush off. Repeat if necessary, moistening the stain with water. Stale stains should be covered with salt moistened with lemon juice; leave until the salt is dry, brush off, then wash. Or rub with glycerine, stretch the stained area over a basin and pour boiling water through it.

Nail Varnish: Nail varnish remover (obvious, but often forgotten in the panic).

Make-up: Lighter fuel or dry cleaning fluid.

Wine: Use the salt and lemon method described for fruit stains.

Blood: Soak in salted lukewarm water.

Ink: Soak in salted lukewarm milk, or rub with a lemon.

Mildew: Soak in salted milk overnight, then wash.

Grass: Sponge with ammonia and water (for white cotton); on other fabrics rub with glycerine, leave for 1 hour, rinse with lukewarm water and wash. Or use methylated spirits.

Paint: Loosen the paint with a blunt knife, then rub with a turpentine-soaked rag.

Oil, tar, grease: Rub with a hand-cleaner such as Swarfega, or use dry-cleaning fluid.

Scorch marks: Mix 2 oz Fuller's earth, 2 oz washing soda, ½ pint vinegar and one finely chopped onion. Put them all into a pan and simmer for 10 minutes. Strain and bottle when cool. Spread on the scorch mark and allow to dry, and re-apply until the mark goes. Rinse and wash.

To take out Mildew — Mix soft soap with starch powdered, half as much as salt, and juice of a lemon; lay it on the part on both sides with a painter's brush. Let it lie on the grass day and night till the stain comes out.

A New System of Domestic Cookery, 1818

Stains of Wine, Fruit, etc after they have been long in the Linen — Rub the part on each side with yellow soap. Then lay on a mixture of starch in cold water very thick; rub it well in, and expose the linen to the sun and air till the stain comes out. If not removed in three or four days, rub that off, and renew the process. When dry, it may be sprinkled with a little water. Many other stains may be taken out by dipping the linen in sour buttermilk, and drying in a hot sun. Then wash it in cold water, and dry it, two or three times a day.

A New System of Domestic Cookery, 1818

Washing grease stains out of man-made fabrics which can only be washed on a cool wash has recently been made much easier by a range of aerosol sprays with very odd names, like Frend (sic), or Shout. These sprays are not only good for grease stains, but others, such as wine, or make-up, and, most important of all, unlike the enzyme powders which damage certain fabrics (and skin), can be used with absolute safety on the most fragile materials — I have recently used them to get rid of a large wine stain on a silk shirt.

Remove fly-marks from fabric lampshades by dusting the marks with powdered french chalk (available from haberdashery departments); then shake together in a bottle 1 table-

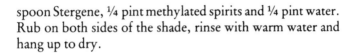

spoon Stergene, ¼ pint methylated spirits and ¼ pint water. Rub on both sides of the shade, rinse with warm water and hang up to dry.

Linen can be bleached by the light of a full moon, as well as by sunlight.

To make fabrics flameproof, rinse them in a solution of 2 oz alum to 1 gallon of water.

Leave cleaner's plastic bags on the wire hangers, and use these when drip-drying shirts. The plastic bag will stop the shirt sticking together and causing creases, and will help it dry more quickly too.

Ironing Sheets

Fold the sheet in half widthways, then fold again in the same direction. Iron both sides of the folded sheet only. As the turn-down is the only part of the sheet which shows, and this is one of the sides to be ironed, then no more ironing is necessary.

Ironing Shirts

Iron the sleeves and cuffs first, then the back, yoke, collar (ironing from each point inwards to avoid those little creases coyly called 'laundry kisses'), and finally the fronts, as they show most. To fold the shirt, do up all the buttons except the second from the top (leaving this undone means that by simply undoing the collar button, the shirt can be pulled on over the head). Lay the shirt front downwards on the ironing board, fold a quarter of the shirt fronts and the sleeves to the back, fold up a third of the shirt, then fold down the top third.

When ironing handkerchieves and table-napkins with some sort of a motif in one corner, make sure that before you start ironing, the motif is face down in the top right-hand corner; iron the article, fold the bottom to the top once, then again. Fold from left to right twice, and the motif will end up neatly on top of the folded handkerchief. We were taught this antiquated nicety at school and I've done it automatically ever since.

Always iron embroidery on the wrong side, so that it acquires a good, raised finish.

Use a clean clothes brush dipped in water to sprinkle on over-dry clothes as you iron, unless you have a steam iron.

Do not store starched linen or it will wear out along the folds. Wash the linen, rough-dry it, fold it in blue tissue paper and store in brown paper.

Lavender bags stored among sheets and pillowcases really do add something very special. There is nothing nicer than going to sleep between lavender-scented sheets.

Store pomander balls amongst blankets, as cloves help keep moths away.

Pomanders

To make pomanders you will need oranges, cloves, powdered cinnamon and orris root and a fine metal knitting-needle. Make holes all over the orange and stick in the cloves; do not insert them too close together, or some will be pushed out as the orange dries and shrinks. Roll the orange in the cinnamon and orris root, then leave to dry in an airing cupboard for about 1 month. If you want to make a hanging pomander, stick ½ in wide sellotape round the orange at right angles, fill in the gaps with cloves, remove the tape and you will have neat channels along which to place the ribbon (add this after the orange has shrunk).

☙ Dyeing ☙

I have not given any tips on dyeing fabrics, as clear directions are always sold with the dyes themselves, but I do include a brief list of 'hedgerow' dyes for anyone interested in experimenting with subtle colours; there are several good books on the subject for anyone wanting to experiment further (see over).

The dyes should be made from freshly-gathered materials. 'Mordaunt' the wool first, so that it can absorb the dye, by boiling it with 4 oz of alum and 1 oz cream of tartar. This should not be necessary with cotton.

In each recipe, add just sufficient water to cover the ingredients.

Browns: Rose-hips, the green husks of walnuts (steep these, covered, for as long as possible, then boil for 30 minutes).

Purples and Blues: Bilberries, woody nightshade, elderberries, privet berries, sloes and damsons. 1 lb berries, washed, chopped and boiled, will dye 1 lb wool or cotton.

Red: The roots of lady's bedstraw, chopped, steeped and boiled.

Pink: The inside of the bark of the silver birch, scraped off and left to steep overnight. Simmer until you have a brownish-red liquid.

Yellows: Onion skins, pear leaves, bracken shoots, young heather. Again, allow about 1 lb per pound of fabric to be dyed. A greengrocer will probably be glad if you relieved him of some of his loose onion skins.

To dye White Gloves a beautiful Purple. Boil four ounces of logwood, and two ounces of roche alum, in three pints of soft water till half wasted. Let it stand to be cold, after straining. Let the gloves be nicely mended: then with a brush do over them, and when dry repeat it. Twice is sufficient unless the colour is to be very dark. When dry, rub off the loose dye with a coarse cloth. Beat up the white of an egg, and with a sponge rub it over the leather. The dye will stain the hands, but wetting them with vinegar will take it off before they are washed.

A New System of Domestic Cookery, 1818

Vegetable Dyes by E. Mairet, published by Faber
The Use of Vegetable Dyes by Violetta Thurstan, published by the Dryad Press

Care of Clothes and Accessories

To revive dark woollen fabrics — black and navy blue suits, coats, blazers, etc. Boil a handful of ivy-leaves in enough water to cover for 10 minutes, then lower the heat and simmer for about 2 hours until the liquid is a good, dark colour. Strain the infusion and add 1 tblsp. ammonia to each pint, then bottle and label clearly as it is poisonous. It will keep indefinitely, and is particularly useful for removing the shine from dark cloth. Sponge the shiny areas of the cloth lightly.

To clean and press velvet. Although it is possible to buy a special velvet-pressing board, it isn't really worth it unless you use a lot of velvet in dressmaking too. Sponge the back of the velvet with the ammonia and water solution mentioned earlier, using as little liquid as possible. If you have someone to help you, get them to hold the fabric taut while you pass a warm iron over the back without touching the velvet itself. If you are doing it on your own, stand the iron on its heel and draw the back of the velvet across it, again without touching the fabric.

To Preserve Furs and Woollen from Moths. Let the former be occasionally combed while in use, and the latter be brushed and shaken. When not wanted, dry them first, let them be cool, then mix among them bitter apples from the apothecary's in small muslin bags, sewing them in several folds on linen, carefully turned in at the edges, and keep from damp.

A New System of Domestic Cookery, 1818

To clean dark fur. Spread the fur out on a newspaper. Heat about 1 lb bran in a warm oven until it is hot enough to handle comfortably. Sprinkle the fur thickly with the bran and work it into the fur with a soft cloth — the warm bran will absorb the dirt, and can be shaken out of the fur out-of-doors. Give the fur a final brush to get rid of any surplus bran.

To clean white or pale fur. Sprinkle with Fuller's earth, rubbing it in with a cloth, as above. Leave for an hour, then shake to remove the powder and brush with a soft brush (a baby's hair-brush is ideal).

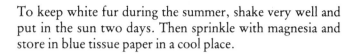

To keep white fur during the summer, shake very well and put in the sun two days. Then sprinkle with magnesia and store in blue tissue paper in a cool place.

Do not store fur with moth-balls. There are now other moth preventives available that do not contain camphor. Cloves, pepper and dried walnut leaves are old-fashioned remedies against moth which smell pleasant. Make sachets containing all three if you have time. Tuck a sachet into each pocket, and hang another round the neck of the coat hanger, wrap the whole garment up in an old sheet, tack up the openings, then hang in a cool, dark place for the summer.

Hang fur ties up by one end, so that the fur flows downwards.

When clothes are subjected to cigarette smoke or cooking smells, hang them in the fresh air before putting them away. An air deodoriser (one which absorbs smells, but doesn't smell itself), is a useful thing to keep in the wardrobe.

Hang pomander balls (page 91), or lavender bags among the clothes in a wardrobe. Or fit a man-size tissue over each hanger hook and sprinkle it with a few drops of your favourite scent. When the scent becomes stale, change the tissue and add fresh scent.

To clean suede shoes, gloves and handbags, make a paste of bran and dry-cleaning fluid and cover the suede with this. Leave it to dry, brush off, then rub with a clean, damp cloth. Do this outside, or near an open window.

Clean suede collars and cuffs with a baby's hairbrush dipped in lighter fuel, brushing until the grease disappears.

Kid gloves can be cleaned with an ordinary pencil rubber — a new one, if possible, to avoid the risk of making the gloves dirtier than ever. Put the gloves on and rub the dirty bits with the rubber. There is a special glove shampoo available, but only use it if you are sure that your gloves are made of washable leather.

Sheepskin gloves and mittens can be washed like sheepskin rugs (page 53), but wear the gloves and wash them on your hands, squeezing your hands together gently. Rinse very thoroughly, squeeze gently to get rid of as much water as possible, then push a wooden spoon up into each glove or mitten, stand the handle in a bottle, and put the gloves to dry in the open air if you can, rubbing them gently as they dry, so that they don't harden.

To dye Gloves to look like York tan or Limerick, according to the deepness of the Dye. Put some saffron into a pint of soft water boiling-hot, and let it infuse all night; next morning wet the leather over with a brush. The tops should be sewn close, to prevent the colour from getting in.

A New System of Domestic Cookery, 1818

Before the winter starts in earnest, give your shoes and boots a good dubbining. Apply it when you take the shoes off so that the warm leather absorbs the dubbin. Leave it on in a thick layer overnight, and next morning wipe off any surplus and polish as usual — you won't have a very shiny pair of shoes, but, if you repeat the dubbining at frequent intervals, you will have dry feet, even in fashionable boots.

To Preserve Boots Watertight in Snow. Rub the crevice between the sole and upper with 'dubbing' and apply a little linseed or castor oil to the sole and upper part.

Household Work and Management, 1910

To remove snow-stains, dissolve a piece of washing-soda in a little hot milk. Spread this mixture on the shoes and leave to dry. Brush, then polish.

Victorian weather-proofing for boots and shoes. Mix neats'-foot oil (from saddlers) with melted beeswax to a cream, colouring it with drawing ink to match the shoes. This is a very good way of protecting children's school shoes from getting scuffed, too, applying it first when the shoes are new, then at monthly intervals.

Rub brown shoes every morning with the inside of a banana skin, and polish with a cloth. Use brown shoe polish once a week.

To soften new leather shoes, warm them near a radiator, then rub in castor oil. Wear the shoes round the house, to help the leather absorb the oil, then polish as usual.

Shoe trees can be made from old socks. Put the socks into the shoes and fill with sawdust or bran, packing well. Cut off the tops of the socks about ¾ in above the tops of the shoes, and sew or staple them together firmly. These are fairly useful for drying out damp shoes, as both sawdust and bran will absorb the moisture; dry out the shoe trees before re-using.

Boot trees made of plastic are useful but expensive. Roll a magazine or newspaper into a thickness which will occupy the leg of the boot, and sellotape in position. Wrap each roll in a polythene bag, tying the bag in a tuft at the top. Push these into the boots when you take them off, and they can easily be pulled out by the polythene tuft.

Wrap white satin shoes in blue tissue paper to prevent them yellowing. Clean with dry-cleaning fluid.

Clean dark velvet shoes and slippers with sticky tape, as suggested on page 81.

To clean pale straw hats, brush with Fuller's earth. Make sure all the powder is out before brushing over with lightly beaten egg-white to give gloss and stiffness. This is a Victorian tip which is just as useful today.

To clean black straw hats, mix 1 teaspoon permanent black ink with 10 drops liquid gum (the kind which comes in a waisted bottle with a red rubber applicator) and brush over the hat.

To clean men's hats, brush thoroughly, then remove grease stains with dry-cleaning fluid. Sprinkle with ground rice or bran, leave 15 minutes and brush off. To prevent grease coming through the crown, put a strip of blotting paper inside the lining.

Getting up black lace. Mix ¼ pint cold tea with 1 tablespoon gum water. Dip the lace into this, squeeze it out, pin it to a flannel-covered board wrong-side upwards, and, when nearly dry, it should be ironed. Black veils may be freshened in the same way.

Household Work and Management, 1910

To revive silver braid or lace, rub on a little dry, powdered magnesia; leave for a few hours and brush off with a plate brush.

To clean ribbons which are not nylon, sponge with 2 teaspoons of ammonia in ½ pint water. Iron with a dry cloth over them until dry.

To give a gloss to silk ribbons, add 1 tablespoon methylated spirits to 1 pint cold water and sponge. Iron as above.

Rejuvenate antique black silk by sponging it with slightly diluted stale beer. Iron on the wrong side.

If you have a precious cobweb wool shawl you daren't wash, it can be cleaned as follows: spread out the shawl on a cloth and sprinkle it with powdered starch. Fold and sprinkle more starch at each fold. Leave for a few hours, then rub gently and shake off the starch. To store the shawl, wrap it in blue tissue paper, then in newspaper, sealing all the joins with sellotape (moths are supposed to dislike printers' ink, and this is a good method of storing any clean woollens). Label clearly.

Lad's love (*Artemisia abrotanum*) was also called 'garde-robe', and was dried and used as a moth-repellant.

✥ *Sewing* ✥

The dressmaker's yard: stretch out one arm and the distance from the tip of the nose (facing forwards) to the tip of the out-stretched index finger is roughly one yard. From the tip of the thumb to the first joint is approximately one inch. One metre can be estimated by adding three thumb inches to one arm's yard. All this quite useful at sale time, or when buying remnants.

Re-use babies' matinée jackets as warm vests by sewing the coat part of the way up the front, leaving an opening big enough to go over the baby's head. Sew buttons and loops to either side of the opening.

When sewing on coat buttons, put a matchstick between the button's holes and sew over it. Remove the match, pull up the slack and wind thread round under the button to form a strong shank. For smaller buttons on shirts etc, replace the matchstick with a pin.

Sharpen scissors by cutting emery or fine sand-paper. Needles and pins can be sharpened and de-rusted by pushing them through sand-paper 2 or 3 times.

Sharpen sewing-machine needles, especially while sewing man-made fibres which blunt the needles very quickly, by running several inches of fine sand-paper through the machine. It is essential to keep needles sharp while sewing artificial fabrics, or the seams may pucker.

Keep dressmaker's chalk in the same box as the pins, to prevent them rusting.

A war-time tip: broken needles can be made into pins with a blob of sealing-wax. Although this is somewhat fiddly, it does make usefully long pins for pile fabrics.

Before sewing tough fabrics like leather, PVC or denim, grease the needle lightly by drawing it alongside your nose (like the carpenter's tip on page 67).

102

Sewing fine jersey is easy providing you buy ball-point needles for the sewing-machine, use a shallow zig-zag stitch for the seams, and stretch the fabric very slightly while stitching the seam. These three tips will produce professional, straight seams.

To cut fur, damp the skin side a little and stretch it fur-side down on a board, fastening it down with drawing pins. When the skin is dry, draw the cutting lines on it with chalk or a pencil. Cut with a sharp razor blade, scalpel, or Stanley knife, but not with scissors.

When making up suede and leather, press the seams with a steam iron, through a double-thickness of dry cloth. Do not push the iron, but 'pat' it on the leather.

Try to keep cotton thread for hand sewing; the new synthetic threads never seem to stay threaded through the needle.

Knot the thread before cutting off a length from the reel; this prevents it knotting as you sew. Don't use too long a thread, it rarely saves time as it invariably gets tangled.

Keep a block of beeswax in your work-basket to wax thread for strong sewing, like coat buttons.

To thread a darning needle, loop the wool over the needle and slip it off the sharp end, pinching the loop between your fingers as you slip it off. Feed this pinched loop through the needle's eye.

To re-use wool, wind the unravelled wool into hanks round a chair-back. Tie each hank in three or four places with a contrasting coloured wool, then wash it carefully by hand in lukewarm soapy water, rinsing it thoroughly. Thread an old stocking through each hank and tie it to the line, allowing the weight of the water to straighten the wool as it dries. Too much water will stretch the wool too much, and alter the tension of the yarn, so give each hank a gentle squeeze if it is too wet.

This is a very useful war-time tip, particularly as wool is now so expensive. Nowadays you can add a fabric conditioner to the final rinse to restore the wool's body and softness.

A North country recipe for a best dress, c. 1890:

> A good long sleeve with room at t'elbow,
> A diamond front an' a rounded back,
> Up to t'neck an' down to t'feet,
> A good deep 'em, and a flounce to't.

Re-lining jackets: Use a shirt to replace a worn lining in an otherwise sound jacket. Remove the shirt collar, cuffs and front band, turn it inside out and push the sleeves down the jacket sleeves. Pin all round, matching shoulder seams and side seams of both garments. Trim the surplus on the shirt, leaving ½–¾ in all round to turn in; slip-stitch in place. Terylene/cotton or nylon shirts are particularly good as they will slip on and off easily. If there is an inside pocket in the jacket, cut a slit in the shirt, turn in the edges and slip-stitch to the pocket edge.

Lengthen children's skirts and trousers by inserting a broad band of a contrasting fabric about 3in from the hem, and using the same fabric to trim pockets or waistband to give a more co-ordinated look. But remember not to mix man-made and natural fibres, or you will have problems with washing and ironing.

For jeans which are much too short, cut the legs off just above the knee (bermuda shorts), and at least 8 in above the knee for brief shorts. Fray the edges for the genuine beachcombing look. This is a useful method for dealing with 'dated' jeans, as shorts do not seem to date as quickly.

A Twenties' tip for repairing astrakhan collars and cuffs: Unravel an old knitted garment in the same colour as the place to be repaired (presumably black). Use this wool to repair the worn area, stitching over and over, leaving loops, so that the loops of unravelled, curly wool look like the astrakhan itself.

Turning sheets 'sides to middle' is not as necessary now as it was in the days of cotton and linen sheets. However, I was glad to have this method passed on to me when my 'old-fashioned' sheets wore out, so I include it here before the useful art is lost.

Tear the sheet up the middle, and join the two sides with as flat a seam as you can. Neaten the raw side seams. If the sheets are too far gone for this treatment, they might still be good for pillowcases.

Make worn towels into hand-towels, or even flannels.

❧ *Out of Doors* ❧

The person who admitted to me that gardening makes her
bad-tempered is surely the exception rather than the rule.
Doesn't gardening, even more than music, have 'charms
to soothe a savage breast'? All the same, she had bowls of
bulbs around the house, and raspberries in the back garden.
Gardening has been an English passion for a thousand years,
as the recent V & A exhibition demonstrated, and those
who, like my friend, say they don't enjoy the work still
manage to like plants.

Although fashions in gardens change, from medieval knot
gardens, to liberated parks with sweeping vistas, from
Gertrude Jekyll's controlled disorder to pristine suburban
plots bright with gladioli, the basic principles behind them
remain the same, and most are based on common sense. Our
allotment neighbour is the first to admit this; he is a gardener
of the old school, saving his own seeds, naturally distrustful

of modern hybrids. He grows prize-winning chrysanthemums which are miracles of size and colour, but produces humbler flowers with the same love and care. Last year my border was punctuated with clumps of alyssum and lobelia grown by him, and he has given me plenty of good advice to go with them. 'Don't dig weeds out,' he advises, 'dig them in. They don't like to be buried so they'll die just the same, but they'll do the earth good as they rot.' 'It's the cold winds that'll kill them, not the frost,' as I planted out wallflowers on a clear October day which threatened frost that evening. He was right, it was the cold wind that killed the unprotected plants when it blew in November. His serried ranks of chrysanthemum plants in their beautiful earthenware pots are set outside in the summer; each plant is held rigid by a long bamboo pole. Every day, in the late afternoon, he inspects the ranks, tapping each cane with a stick. If it sounds hollow the soil is too dry and needs water. This is an excellent tip and one I always use now, whether the plant needs support or not, just pushing a bamboo cane into the pot near the edge. All this is no more than common sense, but it takes some time and experience to acquire so there is no harm in writing it down for quicker absorption by new gardeners.

Gardening today is usually a harmonious mixture of flowers, fruit and vegetables; even on a balcony it's possible to have a grow-bag of tomatoes, a tub of strawberries and one of geraniums. The old cottage garden, which contained a pig, a beehive and some hens as well has largely disappeared. The cottager's pig was part of the 'waste not, want not' rural economy which is no longer considered necessary in our throw-away society. All scraps were fed to the pig, and every scrap of the pig fed a large and hungry family, while its manure helped to produce the vegetables cooked with the bacon. This diet lacked excitement, but it was cheap and reasonably nourishing, and still seems preferable to queuing in supermarkets for packaged food. Various friends have tried this cottage economy but without much success — it is always so much easier in the end to buy what you need. There are remnants of this kind of gardening to be found in the most surprising places. Last week I managed to buy a tree-onion at a herb-farm I was visiting and I took it back to a friend who has a pocket garden on a housing estate south of Manchester. She was delighted. She could remember her father had one growing 'next to a clump of lad's love; he must have had quite a herb-garden', but no one would believe in this plant which produced onions at the ends of its leaves. 'But,' she said, 'I'll have to plant it where our duck can't eat it. It's already had the water-lily out of the pond.' It's a lovely timeless picture, herbs, ducks and ponds in suburbia.

ꙮ *Soil* ꙮ

How to tell fertile ground for a garden:

'We have observed that a good Growth of Trees in the adjoining Hedges, is one excellent Rule of judging; and to this may be added the Aspect and Appearance of the Crops upon the Ground; and even of the Weeds. If every Thing appear vigorous in wild Nature, it is a Promise that culturing it will answer yet better.'

A Compleat Body of Gardening, 1757

If you have heavy soil, find out whether you have a mush-room farm near you and buy a load of mushroom compost from it. Mushroom compost is always quite cheap, but there is generally a great deal of it, so make sure you have enough space for the load that will arrive. Dug in, it will lighten the soil considerably.

For light, infertile soil, plant a crop of brown mustard, sown at the rate of 8 oz to 50 square yards. When the crop is mature, and the ground damp and warm, dig it in and leave it to rot down. It will mean that the land is unusable for a season, but it is worth it for the improvement in the soil.

'If the natural Earth be too tough, throw in Ashes; and, if exhausted by repeated Growths, dig in good, mellow and well-rotted Dung; but not too much of this.'
A Compleat Body of Gardening, 1757

Old gardeners are supposed to have removed their trousers and sat on the soil to see if it was warm enough to sow; to avoid embarrassment in town gardens, testing for warmth with your elbow, as you test a baby's water, should be as effective. The temperature of the air is no indication of the temperature of the soil.

Go upon the lande that is plowed, and if it synge or crye or make any noyse under the fete, then it is to wete to sowe. And if it make no noyse and will beare thy horses, thenne sowe in the name of God.
The Book of Husbandry, 1550

If you can get farmyard or stable manure, leave it to weather out in the open, covered with a polythene sack or two, weighted with stones. After at least six months, and preferably longer, use it by burying it well in the ground it is to fertilise, so that any weed seeds it contains will be well smothered. This may seem obvious, but we used it in ignorance as a mulch and had to contend with a bumper crop of weeds.

Mix 1 lb poultry droppings with 1 oz sulphate of potash and 1 oz bone meal, and apply 5–6 oz of this mixture to every square yard as a good general fertiliser. For brassicas (cabbages, sprouts, broccoli, etc) use the poultry manure alone as a surface mulch.

Poultry manure is a good activator for compost too — use a 2 in layer of it for every one foot of compost material.

If you cannot spare valuable growing space for a compost heap, it can be made very effectively in black plastic rubbish sacks. Make holes all over the sacks first with the tines of a garden fork, then pack in the compost material: fallen leaves (avoiding evergreens as they rot so slowly), vegetable matter from the kitchen, wood-ash, sweepings from rabbit and guinea-pig hutches as long as organic matter was used for bedding, etc. After every 6 in of compost material add a generous handful of poultry manure, or sulphate of ammonia, as activators. Continue until the sack is almost full, then tie up the neck securely and store in a shed, cellar or garage for a year.

Include birch leaves if you can in your compost, as they, too, help break down the vegetable matter, and also help to destroy soil diseases.

Leave the roots of peas and beans in the soil for as long as possible after the plants themselves have ceased to be productive, as they provide valuable nitrogen.

Adding bonemeal is one of the best ways of correcting over-acid soil over a long period. It is expensive, but needs only to be dug in about once every three years, at the rate of 3 oz to the square yard. I use bonemeal for roses, lavender and pinks, which otherwise grow reluctantly in our acid soil.

The best Manure for an Orchard is a Mixture of two Parts Dung and one Part Coal Soot. Let this be blended carefully, and spread all over the Ground between the Trees.
A Compleat Body of Gardening, 1757

Do not use fresh soot, as it will burn the plants. Leave it to weather for about six months in a plastic sack punched with holes and with the neck left open, then use it as a mulch (when it will discourage insects), or as a soil-lightener.

Gardeners call potash 'chemical sunshine', and claim it adds colour to flowers and flavour to fruit and vegetables. So add plenty to the soil if you have a shady garden, and particularly if you have a shady town garden.

Bracken is very rich in potash, so if you can get hold of some, dig it in to the soil. Fuchsias appreciate it as a mulch.

Dried bracken is also useful for protecting tender plants and shrubs in the winter; weave it in and out of a fence of pea-sticks round shrubs to protect them from winter winds, and stuff more bracken inside the barrier to protect them from frost.

Apply a summer mulch if you are an absentee gardener, or if your soil is very light, but remember to:
1. Weed thoroughly
2. Water thoroughly before spreading on your leaf mould, grass mowings, etc. If you can apply the mulch after two wet days, so much the better.

🌿 Weeds 🌿

Cut nettles down to the ground the moment they appear; continuous persecution discourages them and eventually they will give up. They are supposed to indicate a fertile soil.

Let your strong bulls turn over the rich soil in the early months of the years lest, later on, weeds stand in the way and take the smile off the face of your crops.

Virgil, *The Georgics*

> Thistles cut in May return next day,
> Thistles cut in June come up soon
> But cut them in July
> And they are sure to die.

Walter of Henley, in the thirteenth century, endorsed this by saying that thistles should not be cut before St John's Day (June 24th).

Dig weeds (before they seed), spent plants and other vegetable matter straight into the soil, rather than adding them to the compost heap, to provide continuous supply of organic matter to enrich the soil.

One acquaintance tells me to dig a deep trench and bury couch grass, another that it is best to expose the roots and let them die on the surface. I suggest you do whatever is easiest on your soil.

❧ *Planting* ☙

Always plant seeds, and seedlings, in damp ground, watering the soil the night before if necessary. This, too, may seem obvious, but it is extremely important. If the soil is too dry, the seeds and plants will need constant watering to start them into germination or growth, if it is too wet the seeds will rot without germinating at all.

> Four seeds in a hole,
> One for the rook and one for the crow
> One to rot and one to grow.

> When elm leaves are the size of a farthing,
> Plant kidney beans in your garden.

By the time the elm leaves are this size (about the same as a new penny), the danger of frost should be over.

Use fibre egg trays to raise seedlings, instead of expensive peat pots. The fibre will rot in the ground in exactly the same way, so that the plants can be planted out without disturbing the roots.

Good Friday is the traditional Old Wives' day for planting potatoes, but if Easter is early, disregard the old wives and wait for warm soil and warm damp air. If you like your potatoes small, then plant your seed potatoes with all their shoots intact. For a crop of large tubers, remove all the shoots, except for the two strongest nearest the top. If the seed potatoes are very large, cut them in half lengthways before leaving them to sprout.

If you live in sheep-farming country, gather as much of the wool as you can from hedges and fences and keep it in a sack until you plant your runner beans. Then dig a trench, put the wool at the bottom, water it very thoroughly, cover it with about 4 in of earth, then plant the beans as usual. The wool will hold the moisture essential to runner beans, especially in a dry summer, and the lanolin and dung in the wool will act as fertilisers.

Lots of newspaper, torn into strips and saturated with the hose, can be used in the same way as the sheep's wool for runner beans, but you will have to add extra nourishment.

There is not anything superior to the Effect of old Woollen Rags, for the Encouragement of fresh planted Trees.
A Compleat Body of Gardening, 1757

John Hills goes on to explain that the rags should be put in with the roots of the tree at planting, and used as a mulch, held down with stones.

116

❧ Companion Plants ❧

The subject of companion plants is a very interesting one, and worth reading about in much greater detail. I shall only give here the tips that have been passed on to me by word-of-mouth:

Do not plant potatoes too near apple trees.
Keep onions away from runner beans.
Garlic should be kept apart from peas and beans.
Plant peas next to potatoes, leeks and chives next to carrots, carrots next to beans.
Dill is helpful to lettuce and onions, and chervil to radishes.
Plant camomile next to sickly plants.
Leave dead-nettle (*Lamium album*) if you find it growing in the vegetable garden, as it is sympathetic to most vegetables.
Plant mint as an insect repellent, especially against ants.
Grow nasturtiums up the trunks of apple trees, against aphis.
Use oak leaves as a mulch to protect plants against slugs and snails.
Use pine-needles as a mulch for strawberries.
Do not hedge rose beds with box, or the roses will object.
Do hedge a vegetable garden with lavender — any of the aromatic herbs are particularly beneficial to brassicas.
Store root vegetables and apples with maple leaves during the winter. The maple acts as a preservative.
Do not store apples and carrots too close together, or the carrots will become bitter.

❧ Pests ❧

Jeyes' Fluid is a cheap and effective way of controlling most garden pests. Use it as a spray for blackfly, greenfly, etc. and in the watering-can to water round plants to protect from slugs and snails. It is also effective for sterilising greenhouse soil, but not, apparently, for more than three years in succession, as the phenols in the soil will build up to such a degree that, during warm weather, they will rise to the surface and damage the plants (a tip from the Head Gardener of one of Cheshire's finest gardens).

To prevent ants damaging wall-grown fruit:

'Open a little Trench with a Hoe just under the Wall and pour into it a mixture of Brine and Soot. This is very hateful to the Ant, and will be far from damaging the Tree; for it will serve as a Manure to improve its Vigour.'

A Compleat Body of Gardening, 1757

Sprinkle whole cloves, or oil of cloves, round areas infested with red ants. Boiling water poured into an ants' nest destroys the eggs, too; brutal but effective.

An elderflower infusion makes a good anti-caterpillar spray. Infuse about 10 flower heads in 4 pints of water, cool, then strain. When spraying slippery-leafed plants, add a few drops of washing-up liquid to make the spray stick to the leaves.

Slugs:

'The best Instrument for their Destruction is a little Paddle, with a Handle five Foot long, and the Blade sharp. A Blow with this cuts the naked Snail asunder; and he is the worst Enemy the Gardener has. If destroy'd upon the Bed, they should be suffer'd to remain and consume there; for their Flesh soon dissolves into a kind of slimy Moisture, which is wash'd into the Ground by the next Rains, and is a very rich Manure.'

A Compleat Body of Gardening, 1757

Slug pellets can be dangerous in a garden where there are small children and pets. Instead, smear lettuce or cabbage leaves with lard and dot them round the garden. When the leaves are covered with slugs, dispose of them as you like. Of course, if your dog is a Labrador, it will dispose of the cabbage leaves, lard, slugs and all.

To protect dahlias from earwigs, dip a piece of cotton wool in machine-oil and tie it round the stem of the plant, about one foot from the ground. Tie a similar piece round each of the supporting canes as well, or the earwigs will climb those to reach the flowers.

'An Excellent Way to Take Moles, and to Preserve good ground from such annoyance. Put Garlick, Onions or Leeks into the mouths of the holes, and they will come out quickly, as amazed.'

The Enrichment of the Weald of Kent, 1675

To keep rabbits out of your garden, plant only:

Rosemary	R
Azaleas	A
Bluebells	B
Box	B
Iris	I
Tulips	T
Bay	B
Asters	A
Nasturtiums	N

Rabbits are supposed to dislike all these plants.

Use small branches of holly, gorse or any other really prickly shrubs to protect newly-sown seed from mice and birds. Spread the branches flat over the drills, and anchor them with more branches stuck upright.

❧ *Cuttings* ☙

Take geranium cuttings from plants which are flowering well, in July and August, if you want them to flower the next season. This is a better time to do it than the spring.

When taking rose cuttings, choose shoots the thickness of a pencil and about 10 in long. Cut just below a budding 'eye'.

Make a slit about 1 in long in the base of the stem and insert a grain of wheat. The germination of the wheat accelerates the rooting of the cutting.

Take fuchsia cuttings as follows: fill a jam jar with water, and fit a foil cap over it with a rubber band, make a hole in the top and slip the fuchsia cutting through this, to form its roots in the water.

When taking cuttings of any shrubs, plant them round the edges of a flower-pot of sand, or sandy loam. Tie a polythene bag over the pot and cuttings as soon as possible, to avoid transpiration of moisture from the leaves. The cuttings should be ready to plant out a year from taking them. Dipping the end of the stem in hormone rooting powder before planting them in the pot is a help, but not essential.

☙ *Other tips* ❧

Encourage mistletoe to graft itself in your garden by keeping a sprig left over from Christmas in a cold shed until the spring, by which time the berries will have ripened. Cut notches in the underside of branches of apple, poplar or hawthorn trees, and squash a berry into each notch, if necessary binding it in place with an old stocking, or a pair of tights. Growth should appear in the spring of the following year.

Mark clumps of 'blind' spring bulbs, so that, when the foliage has died down, in the late summer and autumn, you can dig them up and replant them singly, to flower the next spring.

Prune weak roses harder than robust ones, and prune newly-planted roses very hard.

Roses to plant if you want to make pot-pourri:

The Rose red, Damask, Velvet, double Province Rose, the sweet Musk-Rose double & single, the double & single white-Rose . . .

A New Orchard and Garden, 1676

Almost all old-fashioned roses make good pot pourri, as they have the richest scent. The rose-garden at Castle Howard, Yorkshire, opened in 1978, provides plenty of ideas when visited at the height of its glory in mid-July, and good stockists of old roses can be found at the end of this chapter.

From the *Smallholder's Year Book for 1923*, a tip on pollinating fruit:

If you have only one variety of apple, plum or pear in your garden, introduce the pollen of a 'foreign' variety by putting

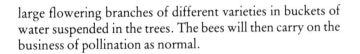

large flowering branches of different varieties in buckets of water suspended in the trees. The bees will then carry on the business of pollination as normal.

Re-tread newly-planted shrubs and herbaceous plants into the earth after the first frost, as the roots may have been pushed clear to the ground. If you don't do this, the next frost will be able to attack the roots and kill the plants.

Never walk over frosted lawns, as it kills the grass, and you will have a trail of brown footprints in the spring.

Seeds must be gathered in fair weather at the Wain of the Moon & kept some in Boxes of Wood, some in bags of Leather & some in Vessels of Earth, & after to be well cleansed & dried in the Sun or shadow. Othersome, as Onions, Chibols & Leeks, must be kept in their husks.

The English House-Wife, 1615

> If the sun shines through the apple trees upon
>   a Christmas Day,
> When autumn comes they will a load of fruit
>   display.

Use an old rubber hot-water-bottle to make a garden kneeling-mat: cut off the neck and open out the bottle by cutting round the side seam. Stick a piece of foam rubber to the inside as padding, then cover it with a non-slip material.

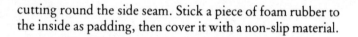 *Indoor Plants*

Never throw away house bulbs. Leave them to dry out after flowering, in a dry shed during the summer, then plant out in the garden in the autumn. Hyacinths will not be as large and vigorous, but will perhaps be the prettier for that.

Add a little charcoal to the soil when planting anything in pots, to keep it sweet.

Under, rather than over, water house plants during the winter, especially if you are going away and leaving the house unheated.

Use an old washing-up liquid bottle as a most accurate watering can for indoor plants.

The Weather

Last year one newspaper reported that 'just as reliable as the weathermen in the short term was the farmers' and sailors'

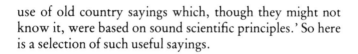

use of old country sayings which, though they might not know it, were based on sound scientific principles.' So here is a selection of such useful sayings.

These are the general prognostics of rain: when cattle snuff the air and gather into the corner of the field with their heads to the leeward, or take shelter in the sheds — when sheep leave their pastures with reluctance — when goats go to sheltered spots — when asses bray frequently and shake their ears – when dogs lie much about the fireside and appear drowsy — when cats turn their backs to the fire and rub their faces — when pigs cover themselves more than usual in litter . . . when moles throw up hills industriously — when toads creep out in numbers — when frogs croak — when bats squeak and enter houses — when singing birds take shelter — when the robin approaches near the dwellings of man — when swans fly against the wind — when bees leave their hives with caution, and fly only short distances — when ants carry their eggs busily — when flies bite severely, and become troublesome in numbers — when earthworms appear on the surface of the ground and crawl about — and when the larger sorts of snails appear.

The Book of the Farm, 1844

'Rain before seven, fine before eleven.' This is more accurate in flat areas than in hilly ones.

A ring round the moon, or the sun, indicates rain; the ring is caused by the moisture in the atmosphere.

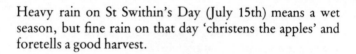

Heavy rain on St Swithin's Day (July 15th) means a wet season, but fine rain on that day 'christens the apples' and foretells a good harvest.

> When the mist is from the hill
> Then good weather it doth spoil.
> When the mist is from the sea,
> Then good weather it will be.

The barometer *falls* for warm, wet, or more wind, and *rises* for cold, dry, or less wind.

> Seagull, seagull,
> Sit on the sand,
> It's never fine weather
> When you're on the land.

This is a very helpful prognostication in coastal areas, when seagulls flying inland indicate bad weather out to sea making its way towards the land.

A heavy dew on a summer morning usually indicates a fine day ahead.

When it is evening, ye say, It will be fair weather: for the sky is red. And in the morning, It will be foul weather today: for the sky is red and lowring.

Matthew 16:2

Or:

> Red sky at night, shepherd's delight,
> Red sky at morning, shepherd's warning.

> Mackerel sky and mares' tails
> Make lofty ships carry low sails.

> If Candlemas Day be fine and clear
> We'll have two winters in the year.

Candlemas is February 2nd.

A green sunset denotes a thaw.

My husband was told by a neighbouring farmer that a sticky film on sycamore leaves foretold a hot summer. When asked what caused the film, the farmer replied, 'It's the sun as does it'!

❧ Animals and the Farmyard ❧

'A cold stable makes a well horse.' This applies to dogs, too; the tougher breeds thrive in unheated sleeping conditions, as long as they are dry and free from draught.

127

Hang large bunches of southernwood (*Artemisia*) in kennels, stables and cowsheds in the summer to keep the flies away.

Aug. 28th: . . . My Greyhounds being both very full of fleas and almost raw on their backs, I put some Oil of Turpentine on them, which soon made many of them retire and also killed many more.

Parson Woodforde, 1787

Dosing a cat with any sort of pill is a very difficult job. If your cat likes yeast tablets, and most of them do, simply rub the pill all over with a yeast tablet. Then give the cat one yeast tablet, followed by the yeasty pill, and ending with some more yeast, all in quick succession. This tip works wonderfully with both our cats, and with those belonging to our friends.

Plant rue round a hen run to ward off disease, and add chopped sage and camomile to the hens' usual diet to aid health and good laying.

Two recipes for rations for laying fowls from *The Small-holder's Year Book*, 1973:

1. 4 parts by weight potatoes; 4 parts bran; 2 parts brewers' grains; ½ part lean meat.
2. 3 parts bran; 2 parts pea meal; 3 parts cut clover chaff; 1 part lean meat.

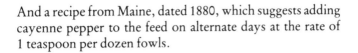

And a recipe from Maine, dated 1880, which suggests adding cayenne pepper to the feed on alternate days at the rate of 1 teaspoon per dozen fowls.

'Twelve to fourteen eggs per day from sixteen hens. If cayenne left out of food for 3 days, number of eggs fell to 4 or 5. This tip is effective for summer as for winter.'

Dr Chase's Recipes, 1880

Tame rabbits are very fertile, bringing forth young every month. As soon as the doe has kindled, she must be put to the buck, otherwise she will destroy her young. The best food for them is the sweetest hay, oats and bran, marshmallows, sowthistle, parsley, cabbage-leaves, clover grass, etc, always fresh. You must be careful to keep them exceeding clean, otherwise they will not only poison themselves, but likewise those that look after them.

The Housekeeper's Instructor, c. 1790

These rabbits were being bred for the table, but the suggestions for feeding and keeping clean are nevertheless good for pet rabbits. 'Marshmallows' are *Althaea officinalis*, now quite rare, so not recommended.

To Prevent the Rot in Sheep. Keep them in the pens till the dew is off the grass.

A New System of Domestic Cookery, 1818

An orphaned newly-born animal will survive for some hours without food as long as it is warm and dry. This is worth

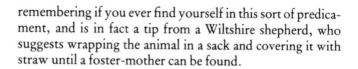

remembering if you ever find yourself in this sort of predicament, and is in fact a tip from a Wiltshire shepherd, who suggests wrapping the animal in a sack and covering it with straw until a foster-mother can be found.

Never walk your dog through in-calf heifers; cows dislike dogs at the best of times, so it is better to give them a wide berth. If they do begin to gather round and look threatening, a sort of breast-stroke gesture with your arms, and a shout or two of 'Hoosh' will usually make them retreat. If there is a bull in with the cows, go the long way round. Make sure of your right-of-way in any case.

Feb. 5th: . . . My poor cow rather better this morning, but not able to get up as yet, she having a disorder which I never heard of before or any of our Somerset friends. It is called Tail-shot, that is a separation of some of the Joints of the Tail about a foot from the tip of the Tail, or rather a slipping of one Joint from another. It also makes all her Teeth quite loose in her head. The Cure, is to open that part of the Tail so slipt lengthways and put in an Onion boiled and some salt and bind it up with some coarse Tape.

Parson Woodforde, 1790

In a word, no cottager's allotment is complete without a pigsty and a good pig; for the pig, first, eats all the refuse; secondly, supplies three or four loads of good dung; and, thirdly, gives not only a relish, but a great addition to boiled cabbage, peas, and beans . . . To recapitulate — the cottager should have:

1. A pigsty, well-drained, well-ventilated in the sleeping compartment, warm and perfectly dry.

2. A well-bred pig. A spayed sow is the best — big enough for flitches.

3. A wife who has education enough, or wit enough to learn how to cure and cook the bacon; even although she may not be able to do crotchet or Berlin wool work.

The Pig, by W. C. L. Martin, 1860

From this invaluable book also comes this memorable sentiment: 'I prefer the grunting of a hog in a cottager's sty to the song of a nightingale.'

Two tips on catching fish, dated 1870; both are said to be irresistible to fish — I wish I could say with honesty that I found them to be so:

1. Mix lovage juice with the bait you are using.

2. Sprinkle the water with a mixture of mullein seed and bread-crumbs.

To prevent green Hay from firing. Stuff a sack as full of straw or hay as possible; tie the mouth with a cord, and make the rick round the sack, drawing it up as the rick advances in height, and quite out when finished. The funnel thus left in the centre preserves it.

A New System of Domestic Cookery, 1818

Spray yards, paths and walls with a strong solution of Jeyes' Fluid to prevent green slime forming on them.

Before the first frosts, paint porous stone and brick with two or three coats of linseed oil, applying the next coat before the first is dry so that as much oil as possible penetrates the stone.

To preserve wood outdoors. Mix 2 parts creosote to 1 part paraffin oil. This can be applied to planed or rough wood, and the effect is distinctly pleasing. It looks as if it has been treated with oak varnish stain. The colour can be regulated by the quantity of paraffin used.

The Smallholder's Year Book for 1923

This mixture also protects the wood against insects, so it is especially useful in poultry houses and pet cages.

❧ *Bees* ☙

When bees swarm on a hot day, a loud noise such as banging of a dustbin lid will make them settle:

> Now dames oft bustle from their wheels
> Wi children scampering at their heels
> To watch the bees that hang and swive
> In clumps about each thronging hive
> And flit and thicken in the light
> While the old dame enjoys the sight
> And raps the while their warming pans
> A spell that superstition plans
> To coax them in the garden bounds
> As if they lov'd the tinkling sounds
> And oft one hears the dinning noise
> Which dames believe each swarm decoys.
>
> *The Shepherd's Calendar*

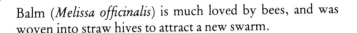

Balm (*Melissa officinalis*) is much loved by bees, and was woven into straw hives to attract a new swarm.

> A swarm of bees in May
> Is worth a load of hay;
> A swarm of bees in June
> Is worth a silver spoon;
> But a swarm of bees in July
> Isn't worth a butterfly.

The Man — will save himself best from the Bees if he has no Hair on his Head, and if his Head be rubbed with Vinegar; but if he should happen to be stung, he may apply a Copper Halfpenny to the wounded Part, and holding it there for a Minute or two, it will prevent the Swelling, or any after Pain.

The Country Housewife, 1753

Bee stings are said to be cures for rheumatism and arthritis.

Store of Bees in a warm and dry Bee-house comely made of Fir-boards to sing & sit, & feed upon your flowers & sprouts, make a pleasant noise & sight. For cleanly & innocent Bees, of all other things, love & become, & thrive in an Orchard. If they thrive (as they must needs, if your Gardiner be skilful & love them; for they love their friends & hate none but their enemies) they will, besides the pleasure, yield great profit to pay him his wages.

You need not doubt their stings, for they hurt not whom they know, & and they know their Keeper & acquaintance. If you like not to come among them, you need not doubt them; for but near their store, & in their own defence, they will not fight, & in that case only (& who can blame them?) they are manly & fight desperately.

A New Orchard and Garden, 1676

Old rose stockists:
Scotts Nurseries (Merriott) Ltd, Crewkerne, Somerset TA16 5PL.
David Austin Roses, Bowling Green Lane, Albrighton, Wolverhampton WV7 3HB.

❧ *Health* ❧

Many of the remedies I came across for this chapter were
based more on superstition than on hard knowledge or even
common sense. One friend, now in her sixties, could remember a nanny she'd had as a child, who swore by old
country cures. Sore throats were treated by applying several
cobwebs to the neck and holding them in place with a warm
woollen scarf, and warts by rubbing them with the largest
slug that could be found in the garden. When I asked whether
these had worked, my friend answered wryly that no doubt
the warm scarf was very effective in curing sore throats, and
that although the warts disappeared, her intense dislike of
slugs had not. So it was very hard to sort fact from fiction;
my greatest help was Culpeper. Among his pages I found
factual answers for curious-sounding medicines, like Parson
Woodforde's tonic on page 141. The old-fashioned dispensing chemists were helpful too, particularly the ones in

farming towns where science and old country lore still combine to serve customers wary of doctors' and vets' ointments. The herb ointment on page 136 is an example of a farmer's recipe which was used on his cows and his family.

Our family medicine cupboard is a typical mixture of old and new remedies, dried lime flowers and mint for making infusions, Paracetemol tablets for colds and headaches, witch hazel for sprains, bruises, and for bathing eyes, surgical spirit for blisters and cold sores, and a bottle of Dr Collis Browne for stomach upsets. There are penicillin tablets for sore throats, but a spoonful of honey is just as effective and much nicer, and there are indigestion tablets, but caraway-seed tea sipped as hot as possible works much faster. An old man once told me that his cure for sharp wind-pains (certainly caused by eating the onions he grew raw with his bread and cheese for lunch) was to take one or two equally sharp, very deep breaths; 'Takes yer stomick by surprise, like.' A pillow of 'sleep-herbs' is the nicest and safest remedy for insomnia; I bought my first one, but shall now make my own from a mixture of dried thyme, camomile, lavender, lemon balm and rosemary. We are not averse to doctors' drugs, but feel they are best kept for 'real' illnesses, and not over-used for colds and flu.

❧ *Infusions, teas and tonics* ❧

I have included the Latin name wherever there might be a slight confusion over identification and, of course, there are many other herbs which produce beneficial teas; any good herbal will give a full list. The recipe for all these teas and infusions is as follows: put a handful of the leaves or flowers in a teapot and cover with 1 pint of boiling water. Allow to stand for about 5 minutes before drinking (for a tea) or

10 minutes before straining and cooling (for an infusion).
If you do not grow these herbs in your garden, most
health food shops and some chemists stock the dried
products.

Important. A stronger tea or infusion does not mean a
quicker cure, but may mean an upset stomach.

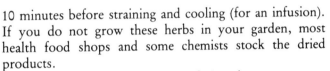

Agrimony (*Agrimonia eupatoria*): an infusion aids diges-
tion and is good for liver complaints; the wine helps
rheumatism.

Angelica (*Angelica archangelica*): an infusion made from the
leaves, benefits those suffering from wind.

Balm (*Melissa officinalis*): the tea is good for colds and
catarrh.

Basil (*Ocimum basilicaum*): an infusion is good for colic.

Beetroot: the wine was taken for anaemia.

Blackberry: an infusion of the leaves is taken cold night and
morning as a general tonic.

Blackcurrant: a tea from the leaves sipped hot relieves hoarse-
ness and sore throats.

Cabbage: the water in which cabbage has been cooked can
be taken cold as a laxative.

Caraway: hot caraway seed tea is very good for indigestion.
Sip it as hot as possible.

Camomile (*Anthemis nobilis*): a cold infusion can be taken as a spring tonic. A hot infusion is good for indigestion, headaches, insomnia and nervous disorders.

Clover (*Trifolium pratense*): the wine is good for 'chestiness'.

Comfrey (*Symphytum officinale*): an infusion is helpful for dysentry.

Dandelion (*Taraxacum officinale*): take the wine for liver complaints.

Elderberry: wine for colds.

Elderflower: tea taken hot at night to promote sleep.

Feverfew (*Tanacetum parthenium*): infusion taken for migraine and headaches, colic and indigestion.

Goldenrod (*Solidago virgaurea*): tea to cure violent sickness.

Holly: leaf infusion, a wineglassful 2–3 times a day was thought to be a preventative against rheumatism.

Lime flowers (*Tilia vulgaris*): tea is good for insomnia, and will also promote sweating to cure fevers.

Mallow (*Althea officinale*): a tea from the flowers, with a little honey, is good for an infected throat or mouth.

Mullein (*Verbascum*): an infusion made from the flowers or leaves is good for coughs, bronchitis and related chest troubles.

Nettle (*Urtica dioica*): tea helps rheumatism.

Parsley: wine for clearing the blood, infusion as an iron tonic.

Rosemary: tea is good for indigestion and headaches.

Sage: and lemon tea helps the complexion. A cold infusion can be used as a mouthwash for tender gums, and a stronger infusion helps the growth of the hair and restores fading colour.

Speedwell (*Veronica officinalis*): take the tea for gout.

Spinach: the water drained from cooked spinach can be used as a powerful iron tonic. Not recommended for those who cannot take strong doses of iron.

Strawberry: leaf tea is useful for mild diarrhoea in small children.

Toast: tea. Pour boiling water over a very brown (not burnt) slice of toast. Leave to infuse until cool, strain and sweeten with a little honey. Curiously refreshing for coughs and flu, and soothing for sore throats. Charlotte Brontë mentions it as part of Louis Moore's cure in *Shirley*.

Watercress (*Nasturtium officinale*): use a strong infusion, cooled, to bathe cuts and grazes.

Yarrow (*Achillea millefolium*): leaf tea. A cup night and morning helps head colds. A cold infusion is good for the hair.

❧ *Health Drinks and Restoratives* ❧

Fruit Salts

4 oz Epsom salts	4 oz cream of tartar
8 oz bicarbonate of soda	4 oz tartaric acid
2 oz citrate magnesia	1¼ lbs caster sugar

Mix all together and sieve three times. Put into a dry jar and cover tightly. Take two teaspoons in water.

Mary Coward, Cockermouth, Cumbria, 1922

Health Lemonade

7 lemons	1 oz citric acid
1 oz tartaric acid	1 oz Epsom salts
3½ lbs sugar	10 breakfastcupfuls boiling water

Mix the sugar, salts and acids. Add the grated rinds of the lemons, then the lemon juice. Pour the boiling water over all, stir and allow to stand for six hours. Lastly, strain through a muslin bag and bottle for use. Dilute with tap or soda water, according to taste, when required. An inch of the cordial in a glass of water makes a splendid drink.

Kirkbride Women's Institute, c. 1930

Tonic Stout

8 oz black malt	2 medium potatoes
1 oz hops	2 oz brown sugar
1 oz dried nettles	1 oz yeast
¼ oz black liquorice	10 pints water

Bring the water to the boil, add hops and nettles, malt, liquorice and the well-washed unpeeled potatoes, pierced

140

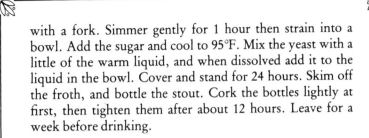

with a fork. Simmer gently for 1 hour then strain into a bowl. Add the sugar and cool to 95°F. Mix the yeast with a little of the warm liquid, and when dissolved add it to the liquid in the bowl. Cover and stand for 24 hours. Skim off the froth, and bottle the stout. Cork the bottles lightly at first, then tighten them after about 12 hours. Leave for a week before drinking.

March 7th: . . . I have taken for these last three mornings one hour before breakfast the second rind of Alder Stick steeped in water, and I do really think that I have gained great benefit from it, half a pint each morning; it must be near the colour of Claret wine. NB very good to take every Spring and Fall.

Parson Woodforde, 1767

The clue to Parson Woodforde's 'tonic' can be found in what Culpeper says about it, bearing in mind Woodforde's interest in food:

The fresh green bark taken inwardly provokes strong vomitings, pains in the stomach, and gripings in the belly, yet if the decoction may stand and settle two or three days, until the yellow colour be changed black, it will not work so strongly as before but will strengthen the stomach, and procure an appetite for meat.

Mrs Beeton's Brandy and Egg Mixture
'One of the most powerful and palatable restoratives.'

2 oz best brandy	Yolk of 1 egg
2 oz cinnamon water	¼ oz sugar

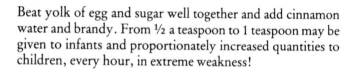

Beat yolk of egg and sugar well together and add cinnamon water and brandy. From ½ a teaspoon to 1 teaspoon may be given to infants and proportionately increased quantities to children, every hour, in extreme weakness!

Thick cream was often prescribed for thin and ailing children, old people and consumptives.

Borage has long been used as restorative herb 'for those that are weak in long sickness', and is included in many drinks of a refreshing and reviving nature. Here is one recipe, useful in the summer to restore energy to flagging tennis players. Make a weak mixture of 1 part white wine to 5 parts water. Add lightly crushed borage sprigs, and lemon slices, then chill in the fridge.

A Diet Drink
Take Figs, and Raisins sliced, of each four Ounces, Anni-seeds and sweet Fennel bruised, of each three Ounces, Liquorice Two Ounces, Cinque foil, two handfuls, Mallow-roots and Fennel-roots, of each three Ounces; boil them in Four Quarts of Water for a Quarter of an Hour, then strain it, and sweeten with Sugar-candy. When it is cold, put it in Bottle, and drink it three times a Day.

The Country Housewife, 1753

A Hangover Cure
Mix the juice of a freshly-squeezed orange or lemon with a large spoonful of honey, and add two ice cubes. Repeat every hour.

142

A Soothing Bedtime Drink for a Cough

Stir a large teaspoonful of black treacle into a cup of hot milk, then add a sprinkling of nutmeg. Drink this in bed.

Mrs Beeton's Restorative Jelly

1 lb shin beef	1 quart cold water
1 ox foot	½ teaspoon salt

Wash and blanch foot and divide into small pieces. Cut beef into small pieces, place it with the prepared ox foot, water and salt in a jar with a close-fitting lid, and cover with 3 or 4 folds of greased paper. Have ready a saucepan of boiling water; in it place the jar and cook slowly for at least 7 hours. Then strain, skim, season to taste and pour into a previously wetted mould. Also excellent warmed as soup.

Lavender Drops

Stir as many lavender flowers into a cup of brandy as the brandy will absorb. Cover and leave for a fortnight. Strain and add a pinch of ground cloves. Take six drops on a lump of sugar to relieve nausea or hysteria.

✑ Syrups ✑

Cough Syrup

1½ pints water	2 oz brown sugar
1 oz raisins	2 oz linseed
1 liquorice stick	Juice of 1 lemon and 1 orange

Simmer all the ingredients, except the orange and lemon juice, in a covered pan until you have a strong infusion. Take off the heat, add the citrus juices, stir, strain and cool. Take a tablespoonful three to four times a day, or a dessertspoonful twice a day for young children.

For a Cough and Shortness of Breath

Take Elecampane-roots one Ounce; Saffron, a quarter of an Ounce; Ground-Ivy and Hyssop, of each one Handful; boil these in two Quarts of Water, till above half is consumed; strain it out, and sweeten it with Sugar-candy, and take three spoonfuls often.

The Country Housewife, 1753

Coltsfoot Syrup (Tussilago farfara)

Boil the leaves with enough water to cover. Strain and add 12 oz sugar to each pint of infusion and simmer to make a syrup. Very good for coughs and sore throats.

Coltsfoot Candy

Coltsfoot candy is also very good for coughs, and very pleasant. Take one pint of the strong infusion made as above and put in a pan with 1 lb sugar, 1 lb golden syrup and a small nut of butter. Boil until it makes a hard ball when dropped in cold water, then pour into an oiled tin and mark into squares when almost cold. Wrap in waxed paper.

Sunflower Syrup for Coughs
Crush 2 oz ripe sunflower seeds and boil for 10 minutes with 1 pint water and 8 oz sugar. Strain and bottle, and take 1 tablespoon for adults, 2 teaspoonfuls for children.

Cowslip Syrup
Infuse 1 lb cowslips in 1½ pints boiling water for 10 minutes. Strain, then simmer with 12 oz sugar until thickened. Take a tablespoonful in a little water at night for nervous debility, and to calm the nerves.

Note: Dried cowslip flowers can be bought from herbalists.

Honeysuckle Syrup for Asthma
Infuse 1 oz of fresh honeysuckle flowers in 1 pint boiling water. Add 8 oz sugar and simmer to make a syrup. Strain and bottle.

Nettle Syrup
Infuse 8 oz young nettle tops in 1 pint water. Strain and add 12 oz sugar, then simmer to make a syrup. Bottle and dilute with cold water or soda water, and drink night and morning as a blood tonic, to clear the skin.

❧ Ointments and Cures ❧

An Ointment for the Piles, when Swelled and Painful
Infuse Elder-flowers in Linseed Oil; let them stand in the Sun a Month; then strain it, and take two Spoonfuls of this

Oil, an Ounce of Beeswax, half an Ounce of Turpentine, the Yolk of an Egg, beat all together in a Mortar, spreat it on a Cloth and apply it to the Part.

The Country Housewife, 1753

Cold Weather Liniment

Mix 1 part oil of cloves with 9 parts camphorated oil and rub into aching muscles, especially after gardening on a damp, cold day.

Soak tired feet in very hot, salty water, to which a few drops of iodine have been added. Dry them and rest for ten minutes with the feet higher than the head.

Mustard Bath

For colds, aching muscles, and after being soaked in bad weather. Add ½ oz mustard powder to 1 gallon hot water. Soak in the bath for fifteen minutes, then dry and put on plenty of warm clothes.

Herb Ointment for Grazes and Bruises

1 lb lard
A good handful of elderflowers, wormwood (*Artemisia absinthum*) and groundsel

Chop the herbs and simmer for half an hour in the melted lard. Strain into pots, and cover when cool. Use fresh herbs for this, and all other ointments.

Buttercup Ointment for all Skin Troubles

Put 4 oz vaseline into a pan with as many buttercup heads as it will absorb. Add more as the vaseline melts. Simmer for 45 minutes, strain while still hot, and cover when cool.

Yorkshire Gorse Salve

Melt 1 lb lard and add as many gorse flowers as the lard will absorb. Leave overnight on the back of the stove or in a very low oven, then next day strain the lard and add another lot of gorse flowers. Repeat the process until the lard is a good yellow from the flowers. Strain and pot.

This salve is used by the fishermen of Whitby to heal hands cracked by salt water and cold weather. It is also good for gardeners, as the gorse heals cuts and thorn wounds.

Embrocation

Put ½ pint turpentine and 1 egg into a bottle and shake hard until creamy. Add 1 pint vinegar and a tablespoon of ammonia to the bottle and shake again.

This will keep for years if well corked, and is reputed to have been used by the early Lake District climbers as a soothing rub for their tired muscles.

Add a small piece of camphor to the above embrocation and it becomes a liniment for chilblains.

Ointment for Chilblains

Mix 2 tablespoons honey, 2 tablespoons glycerine and the white of an egg with enough cornflour to make a paste. Apply after bathing the feet and allow to dry.

You can also rub chilblains with a raw onion, or methylated spirit, or apply a poultice of raw turnip.

To Cure Ring Worms

Get the coomb of a church bell, that is, the grease which is applied to make it work easy, and which, with the metal forms a kind of verdigris; mix it with unsalted lard, and apply a fresh plaster twice a day. It is not superstition that dictated the use of a church bell above any other, but the peculiar combination of metal employed for that purpose produces a different kind of verdigris. This remedy was long kept a profound secret, and many cures effected at an enormous charge.

The Housekeepers' Guide, 1834

❧ First Aid ❧

Bites and Stings

Not omit to mention common salad oil as a sovereign remedy against the bite of the viper.

The Natural History of Selborne, 1789

Francatelli suggests applying a bruised poppy leaf to a wasp sting for immediate relief.

Extract the sting itself if you can, then dab on water and ammonia, or water and soda, or blue-bag.

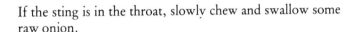

If the sting is in the throat, slowly chew and swallow some raw onion.

The following lotion was taken with them by experienced travellers to Africa and India as an effective cure for mosquito bites. Ask the chemist to make up a solution of carbolic 1–20, then add a few drops of eau de Cologne; dab this on the bite at once.

A weak solution of ammonia and water will also help prevent itching and swelling if applied as soon as possible.

Simples Serving against the Stingings and Bitings of Venomous Beasts:
>   Chicken braines taken in wine.
>   Caterpillars applyed with oyle.
>   Honey drunk with oyle of Roses made hot.
>   Delphiniums applied to the wound.

Simple Serving against the Bitings of Shrew-mice:
>   The shrew-mice themselves cut into pieces applyed to the wound.

The Ladies' Dispensatory, 1651

Cuts, Grazes, Bruises

Apply tinctures of: marigold (*Calendula*) to clean wounds; St John's wort (*Hypericum*) to infected wounds; arnica or witch hazel to bruises; nettle to mild burns; and yarrow to stop bleeding.

Apply a cobweb to a shallow cut to stop the bleeding. This does work extremely well, and it is worth risking censure and leaving the odd cobweb hanging around the house for just such an eventuality.

Mar. 23rd: . . . Memorandum. In shaving my face this morning I happened to cut one of my moles, which bled much, and happening also to kill a small moth that was flying about, I applied it to my mole and it instantaneously stopped the bleeding.

Parson Woodforde, 1779

Bathe a cut with warm water and boracic, then paint with a little medicinal paraffin to keep it sealed from dirt.

Wash grazes gently with warm water and apply antiseptic *cream*. Liquid antiseptic very often dries the skin and makes the graze much more painful.

Rub bruises with butter or, more effectively, with witch hazel or arnica.

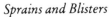

Sprains and Blisters

Soak a pad of lint or cotton wool in witch hazel and bind it over the sprain. Renew the witch hazel as it dries out. This reduces the swelling and is very soothing and highly effective if applied as quickly as possible.

If you have comfrey (*Symphytum officinale*) in the garden, chop a handful of the leaves finely and apply them as a poultice to the sprain; leave this poultice on overnight. Comfrey is a great healer, 'yea, it is said to be so powerful to consolidate and knit together, that if they be boiled with dissevered pieces of flesh in a pot, it will join them together again' (Nicholas Culpeper).

To prevent blisters before a walking holiday or a boating trip, rub the areas likely to be affected with surgical spirit, after a bath, for about a week in advance. Do this every day, and it will harden the skin enough to prevent it blistering.

Deal with blisters, if they do occur after all the precautions, by lancing them with a needle sterilised in a match flame. Gently ease out the fluid, then dab on surgical spirit, which will sting but will harden the raw area so that the skin can heal. The lancing is not painful.

Dab cold sores with surgical spirit.

Soak a slice of bread in vinegar for 2 days and apply a piece to the corn overnight, under a plaster. Every 3 days soak the corn in hot water and peel off the top layer; continue until the corn has disappeared. Or rub with fresh yeast every morning.

The cures for warts are more a matter of folk lore than fact, as it seems whatever cure is followed, the warts will simply disappear in their own good time. However, here are a few suggestions: Francatelli suggests rubbing them with the bruised leaves of the marigold to which a few drops of reduced vinegar have been added; or apply the juice of the greater celandine, the dandelion, the inside of a broad-bean pod, the verdigris from the copper coin, and a black slug, the larger the better.

To draw out thorns and splinters, apply a piece of sticking plaster (preferably the stretch fabric sort) directly over the thorn, pressing the plaster down firmly on the skin. Leave overnight, then peel off the plaster and the thorn should come with it, or at least be so near the surface of the skin that a very little squeezing will persuade it to come out. Only if the splinter is in very deep will you need to apply a second piece of plaster. This is an infallible remedy, taught to us by an *au pair* girl when we were little and used ever since. It is the friction of the plaster on the skin which generates heat enough to draw out the thorn.

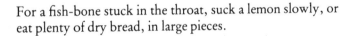

For a fish-bone stuck in the throat, suck a lemon slowly, or eat plenty of dry bread, in large pieces.

Styes

The old wives' tales are many: that the stye should be rubbed with a piece of silk which has first been drawn through a wedding-ring, that it should be rubbed with the wedding-ring itself, without removing the ring from the finger, as that would mean bad luck and hence no cure. Parson Woodforde adds another remedy:

Mar. 11th, 1791: . . . Mem. The Stiony on my right Eye-lid is still swelled and inflamed very much. As it is commonly said that the Eye-lid being rubbed by the tail of a black Cat would do it much good if not entirely cure it, and having a black Cat, a little before dinner I made a trial of it, and very soon after dinner I found my Eye-lid much abated of the swelling and almost free from Pain. I cannot therefore but conclude it to be of the greatest service to a Stiony on the Eye-lid. Any other Cats Tail may have the above effect in all probability — but I did my Eye-lid with my own black Tom Cat's Tail.

In fact the cure was not totally successful and he resorted to a 'plaister', and finally warm milk and water.

The method we use at home I learnt from a friend with whom I shared a flat, and which was later endorsed by our optician. It doesn't prevent a stye, but hastens the cure. Bind a pad of cotton wool to the bowl of a wooden spoon with a large cotton handkerchief (the idea is to have as much

153

material as possible to absorb the hot water and make a more effective poultice), and pour boiling water into a pudding basin. Stand the spoon in the hot water for about 2 minutes, then hold it as close to the eye with the stye as possible, without actually touching the stye itself. Repeat this as often as you can during the day. At night, it is a good idea to apply an ointment bought from the chemist to stop the infection spreading along the eyelid.

Toothache

Tie up a large handful of salt in a handkerchief and heat it in the oven until hot enough to bear but not burn. Hold it against the face until the salt cools and re-apply if necessary; this remedy is also excellent for earache.

Use camomile instead of salt; dried camomile flowers are widely available from herbalists, health food shops and chemists, and are particularly suitable if the pain is the result of a tooth extraction. The substance (azulene) formed when the essential oil is distilled from camomile is anti-inflammatory and therefore good for muscular aches and pains. Heating the camomile releases some azulene to help reduce the swelling and the pain.

Oil of cloves can be applied to the aching tooth (it numbs the taste-buds, however).

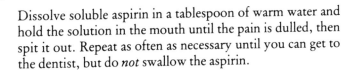

Dissolve soluble aspirin in a tablespoon of warm water and hold the solution in the mouth until the pain is dulled, then spit it out. Repeat as often as necessary until you can get to the dentist, but do *not* swallow the aspirin.

Bleeding

Periwinkle — its Government and Virtues. Venus owns this herbs and saith, That the leaves eaten by man and wife together cause love between them. The Periwinkle is a great binder, stays bleeding both at mouth and nose, if some of the leaves be chewed.

The Complete Herbal, 1653

A cold key dropped down the back, inside the clothing, is thought to stop a nose-bleed, the shock of the cold metal being the cure. I cannot really say if this works, but lying flat on the floor (with a box of paper handkerchiefs to hand) certainly seems the best way of dealing with one.

Inflammation of the Joints, Muscles and Nerves

Arthritis: Rub the affected joints with vinegar; it helps to ease the pain, and is also a preventive.

Rheumatism: Carry a potato or a nutmeg in a hip pocket, or wear a cast-off snake skin as a garter. A little camphor dissolved in methylated spirits and rubbed into the affected parts is beneficial, and a small quantity of powdered sulphur worn in the foot of socks or stockings and renewed every four days is considered an effective preventive.

Lumbago: Sprinkle a little turpentine on a piece of thick, soft fabric, place it over the affected area and lie down for half an hour (no longer, or the turpentine might cause blistering). The embrocation on page 147 is also helpful.

Sciatica: John Wesley's cure: 'Boil nettles till soft. Foment with the liquor, then apply the herb as a poultice. I have known this cure a SCIATICA of forty-five years standing.'

Culpeper's cure for the same: The pounded seed of white mustard (*sinapis alba*) mixed with breadcrumbs and vinegar and applied with advantage to old rheumatic and sciatic pains. Or, carry a tiny bottle of mercury in a hip pocket.

Neuralgia: Heat brown paper, dip it in vinegar, sprinkle it with pepper and bind it round the face with a woollen scarf.

Hot witch hazel, applied with a pad of cotton wool brings relief too.

Headaches: Vinegar applied to the forehead with cotton wool can cure a headache.

Stomach Disorders

For indigestion, take three drops of oil of peppermint mixed with one tablespoon rum, gin, brandy or whisky, or sip just-boiled water as hot as you can.

For a sharp attack of wind, take a few quick deep breaths, as deep as you can.

For a bilious attack, mix the juice of half a lemon with ½ teaspoon of bicarbonate of soda and 2–3 tablespoons of boiling water.

1 tablespoon of powdered mustard in half a glass of warm water is a safe and quick emetic.

Car-sickness: Sit the sufferer on a thick pad of newspaper; give plenty of glucose in whatever form it is liked best before and during the journey; attach a chain beneath the car itself, long enough to clear the road surface by only one inch.

Cures of Hiccups

A Powder to stop the Hickup in Man, Woman or Child. Put as much Dill-seed, finely powdered, as will lie on a Shilling, into two Spoonfuls of Syrup of Black Cherries, and take it presently.

The Country Housewife, 1753

Put your fingers in your ears, hold your breath, shut your eyes and swallow three times. An old schoolroom remedy for hiccups which almost always works; shutting your eyes is to stop anyone making you laugh before you have time to swallow enough.

Or, press the thumb of your right hand hard into the palm of your left and hold your breath.

And finally, take a teaspoon of vinegar, or a pinch of salt.

Miscellaneous Remedies

To prevent nappy rash, powder the baby with dry starch. To cure it, rub in honey, or apply a bread poultice.

Use honey for chapped lips and hands, rubbing in until the stickiness disappears. Rub honey on the gums of teething babies; the rubbing soothes the pain and the nice taste makes them forget it for a minute or two.

Thursday, New Year's Eve: Edwin Law told me of an infallible receipt for warming cold and wet feet on a journey. Pour half a glass of brandy into each boot. Also he often carries a large pair of stockings with him to wear over boots and trousers. He has been a long time in Nova Scotia.

The Diary of the Rev. Francis Kilvert.

Simples Serving for the Heart:
  For Surroundings of the Heart, the Smell of Cowcumbers.
The Ladies' Dispensatory, 1651

Hysterics: Light diet, warm clothing, early rising and early retiring, and plenty of occupation are the best general treatment. During a fit of hysterics, the patient should be addressed sharply, no sympathy being offered, but a douche of cold water promised and perfect solitude granted.
Household Work and Management, c. 1910

🌿 *Preventives* 🌿

Nov. 27th: . . . My Brother recommending me last Night to carry a small Piece of the roll Brimstone sewed up in a piece of very thin Linnen, to bed with me and if I felt any Symptom of the Cramp to hold it in my hand or put it near the affected part, which I did, as I apprehended at one time it was coming into one of my legs, and I felt no more advances of it.

Parson Woodforde, 1789

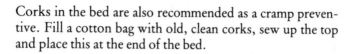

Corks in the bed are also recommended as a cramp preventive. Fill a cotton bag with old, clean corks, sew up the top and place this at the end of the bed.

Against Drunkenness. If you would not be drunk take the powder of Betony and Coleworts mixt together; and eat it every morning fasting, as much as will lye upon a six-pence, and it will preserve a man from drunkenness.

The English Housewife, 1649

To avoid a hangover, drink plenty of water alongside the alcohol, and a least a pint before falling into bed.

To keep off gnats and mosquitoes, smear oil of geranium or oil of pennyroyal over exposed areas of the skin.

To prevent winter chest complaints, in the coldest parts of Northern England, children would be 'sewn into their vests' at the onset of winter and would not be 'unsewn' until spring. Sometimes, a thick layer of goose dripping would be applied to the chest and back, with a layer of brown paper worn over it. Finally would come a good flannel vest, with any draughty openings firmly sewn up.

Garlic and onions are among the best cold preventives, so eat plenty of both in whatever form you can during the winter.

If you like either raw, so much the better (although not necessarily for others; chewing parsley stops your breath smelling as well as being very good for you), but 'garlic pearls' can be bought in health food shops and taken as pills. Culpeper recommends garlic as an interior antiseptic, guarding against disease 'coming by corrupt agues or mineral vapours, or by drinking corrupt and stinking waters'.

May 6th: . . . To 18 Yards of black Ribband of (Bagshaw) pd. 0.5.0. Gave my Brother half my Black Ribband. The Ribband is designed to put round our Necks to prevent sore throats.

Parson Woodforde, 1790

Tobacco was chewed to keep the stomach in good order, and to prevent worms. As tobacco was expensive, once chewed it would be dried and smoked.

A Very Good Way to prevent the Nail growing into the Toe. If the Nail of your Toe be hard and apt to grow round, and into the Corners of your Toe, take a Piece of broken Glass, and scrape the Top very thin; do this whenever you cut your Nails, and, by constant Use, it makes the Corners fly up, and grow flat; so that it is impossible they should give you any Pain.

The Country Housewife, 1753

Receipt against the Plague

Take of rue, sage, mint, rosemary, wormwood and lavender, a handful of each; infuse them together in a gallon of white wine vinegar, put the whole into a stone-pot closely covered up, upon warm wood-ashes, for four days; after which draw off (or strain through fine flannel) the liquid, and put it into bottles well corked; and into every quart bottle put a quarter of an ounce of camphor. With this preparation wash your mouth, and rub your loins and your temples every day; snuff a little up your nostrils when you go into the air, and carry about you a bit of spunge dipped in the same in order to smell to upon all occasions.

The Art of Cookery made Plain and Easy, 1784

❧ *Beauty* ❦

Beauty is as much a minefield of sense and superstition as health. Bathing freckles with morning dew may sound charming, but it would be unfairly misleading to pretend that it was the slightest bit effective. The seventeenth and eighteenth century books like Sir Hugh Platt's *Delightes for Ladies*, published in 1600, or *The Compleat Gentlewoman* by Hannah Wooley, 1711, contain beauty recipes which have quite as much, if not more, sense in them as do modern ones. Women have always been gullible when it comes to cosmetics, and even with modern education are just as likely to believe in a *very* expensive soap 'formulated especially' for individual skins, as they were to believe in Sir Hugh Platt's recipe 'How to Gather and Clarifie May Dew'. There is sound sense in using a rosemary rinse for hair, but little sense in paying large sums for it; it is easy to make if you have rosemary growing in the garden, but just as easy to make from dried rosemary if you haven't.

Many of the old face creams call for difficult and even dangerous ingredients. We raise our eyebrows at the contents of some modern cosmetics, but they are in fact reasonably safe compared with the mixtures of white lead used by Elizabethan ladies to help them attain as white a skin as that of Queen Elizabeth herself. Spermaceti, 'a white fat substance, found in an immense cavity in the skull of the whale' (*A Child's Guide to Knowledge*, 1876), is now mercifully unobtainable, so I have omitted those recipes which call for it, except where white beeswax can be used instead. Beeswax in its golden unpurified form makes a lovely honey-smelling hand cream; use it instead of the white beeswax in the recipe for cleansing cream on page 169.

Some of the best beauty tips are also the simplest. The idea of having a jar of bran to rub your hands in after washing them was given to me by a lady who is great gardener. 'If I had to buy all the hand cream I need to keep my hands reasonable, my pension wouldn't stand it.' She called the bran idea a 'house-maids' tip' — 'they couldn't afford hand-creams either'.

These home-made beauty recipes are particularly useful for people with sensitive skins allergic to the chemicals and scents to be found in most commercial products, but most of them keep only moderately well, so it is best to store them in the fridge in the summer, and make them only in small quantities. The ingredients are all available from dispensing chemists (the most old-fashioned are usually the most helpful), and branches of Culpeper Ltd are also good. Their postal service can be obtained by writing to them at Hadstock Road, Linton, Cambridge.

The following should be in every toilet cupboard:
  Benzoated lard, for chapped hands
  Cocoa butter, to strengthen the eyebrows
  Oil of sweet almonds, for brittle nails
  Fine oatmeal, for softening the water
  Precipitated chalk, as a dentifrice
  Prepared Fuller's earth, as a toilet powder
  White wine, as an astringent wash
  Lavender water, a little to be added to the washing water
  Elder-flower water, for bathing a flushed face.

The Ladies' Realm, 1904

❧ *Lotions* ❧

Sarah Bernhardt's Lotion for the Face
2½ oz alum
1½ fl oz almond milk
6 fl oz rose water

Dissolve the alum in the rose water, add the almond milk and shake well.

Milk of Roses for a Dry Skin
Rose water 1 pint
Oil of almonds 1 oz
Oil of tartar (which must be added last) 10 drops

Shake well together and it will appear exactly like milk.

The Housekeeper's Guide, 1834

Camomile Lotion for Dry Skin
Infuse 8 flower heads in ½ pint boiling water. Bottle when cool and use within one week.

Lemon Lotion for Greasy Skins
Rind of 1 lemon
1 oz powdered borax
2 oz glycerine

Steep the lemon rind in 4 fl oz boiling water. Strain and dissolve the borax in it, then add the glycerine, bottle and shake well.

Skin Freshener
Mix equal parts of rose water and witch hazel. For dry skins substitute orange flower water for the rose water.

Lotion to Reduce Skin Redness
Infuse cucumber slices in rose water, strain and bottle. Bathe the face with this night and morning.

Skin Clearing Lotion
To be taken internally to cleanse the blood or, externally, to cleanse the pores.

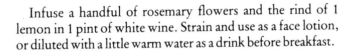

Infuse a handful of rosemary flowers and the rind of 1 lemon in 1 pint of white wine. Strain and use as a face lotion, or diluted with a little warm water as a drink before breakfast.

Milk Lotion for Rough, Red Hands

Put equal quantities of glycerine, milk and surgical spirit into a bottle. Shake well and apply at night.

Tanning Lotion

5 fl oz cold tea	1 tablespoon orange flower
2 tablespoons olive oil	water or triple strength
2 tablespoons lanolin	rose water

Mix the strained tea with the olive oil and lanolin, and add a tablespoon of orange flower water or rose water to scent it a little. This lotion benefits from being made in the blender, which makes it very smooth and thick. It is pleasant to use, but should not be regarded as giving enough protection to skins which burn easily.

Cold tea is a soothing lotion for sunburn.

Rosemary and Sage Lotion for Dark Hair

Use sage leaves and rosemary to make a strong infusion. Leave to cool, covered, strain and bottle. Use it either in the final rinsing water to give a shine to the hair, or dabbed into partings in the hair every morning to improve the scalp.

To Preserve Hair and make it grow thick

Take one quart of white wine, put in one handful of Rosemary flowers, half a pound of honey, distill them together; then add a quarter of a pint of oil of sweet almonds, shake it very well together, put a little of it into a cup, warm it blood-warm, rub it well on your head and comb it dry.

The Art of Cookery, 1784

For Falling Hair in India

The Indian climate frequently causes the hair to fall off. Caster oil and eau de Cologne in equal parts, mixed well, is a good stimulant.

The Young Ladies' Journal, c. 1890

Borax Lotion for Dandruff

Dissolve a teaspoon of borax in 1 cup of warm water. Apply every day to partings in the hair.

❧ Creams ❧

Cold Cream

Warm 4 oz white wax in a bowl over hot water. Beat in 8 oz almond oil, 4 oz elderflower water and a few drops of a favourite scent if required.

Cleansing Cream

Melt 2 oz white beeswax in a bowl over hot water and add
7 fl oz almond oil. Warm together 1 teaspoon borax and
2½ fl oz orange flower water and blend into the wax and oil,
stirring often until cool, to ensure a smooth mixture.

Almond Cleansing Cream

Mix 2 oz ground almonds with 1 teaspoon clear honey, then
add enough milk to make a thick cream. This should be kept
in the fridge and used quickly.

Elderflower Cream for Dry Skin

Melt 1 lb pure lard in a saucepan and add as many handfuls
of elderflowers, stripped from their stalks, as it will absorb.
Simmer gently for about 30 minutes. Strain through a muslin-
lined sieve, then pot.

Almond Paste for Rough and Chapped Skins

This is simple to make and very effective, especially during
the winter for skin exposed to rough weather.

1½ oz ground almonds	1 drop bitter almond oil
About 150 ml rose water	1 drop of a favourite scent

Warm the ground almonds in a bowl over a pan of hot water,
adding enough rose water to make a stiff paste. Remove

from the heat, warm the rest of the rose water and add to the paste until you have a thick cream, then add the bitter almond oil and the scent. I had a little trouble buying bitter almond oil, although I managed to find some in the end; I think ordinary almond oil is as good.

A Paste for Chapped Hands, and which will preserve them smooth by constant use. Mix a quarter of a pound of unsalted hog's lard, which has been washed in common and then rose-water, with the yolks of two new-laid eggs, and a large spoonful of honey. Add as much fine oatmeal, or almond-paste, as will work into a paste.

Domestic Cookery, 1818

Cheap Hand Cream

Mix 1 oz boracic powder with 2 oz vaseline and rub in well. This cream is a good one to use after gardening, as it is soothing and healing.

Lip Salve

Melt 1 oz beeswax with 1 oz almond oil. Add a piece of alkanet root (*Alkanna tinctoria*) and simmer until the salve is a good red, then strain into a small pot. Red food colouring can be used for this, although alkanet can be bought from good herbalists; tinted or not, this is very good for protecting lips in cold weather and is pleasant to use.

A Victorian remedy for freckles, which were regarded as unsightly and 'hoydenish'. Pound 1 part alyssum seeds with 2 parts honey and apply overnight (try grinding the alyssum seeds as finely as you can, or they will be uncomfortable).

To Make Pomatum

Take hog's lard, cut it in small pieces, and soak it 8 days, in spring water, changing it daily, and keeping it covered close all the time. Melt it in a jar, set it in a kettle of hot water. When melted strain it, and stir till it begins to chill; then drop in oil of lavender, or essence of lavender, to scent it; stir well and pour into small gallipots. This is soft pomatum. If to be hard, melt with the lard an equal quantity of mutton suet or marrow, and to four ounces put one quarter ounce of white wax. Strain and scent as above.

The Housekeepers' Guide, 1834

To Breed Hair, take Southernwood, and burn it to ashes and mix it with common oyl; then anoint the bald place therewith morning and evening and it will breed hair exceedingly.

A Little Book of Conceited Secrets

Very easy to make, and worth trying.

❧ *Face Packs and Masks* ❧

Princess Henrietta's Mask

Mix 2 tablespoons powdered orris root with almond oil to

make a thick paste. Allow it to dry on the skin, and remove with tepid water. To whiten a sallow skin, and soften a dry one.

Face Packs for Dry Skins

1. Mix a beaten egg with the strained juice of a lemon. Add enough ground almonds to make a cream. Allow to dry on the face and remove with lukewarm water.

2. Mix fine oatmeal to a paste with almond oil, and use while having a bath, to allow the oil to penetrate the warm skin.

Face Packs for Greasy Skins

1. To equal quantities of peroxide and witch hazel add enough Fuller's earth to make a cream. Leave on the face until dry if the skin is very greasy, or for 5 minutes only if the skin is just slightly oily.

2. Mix fine oatmeal with witch hazel and leave on for 15 minutes.

❧ Bath Condiments ❧

Toilet Soap

1½ lbs clarified fat	4 oz caustic soda dissolved in
½ lb coconut oil	¾ pint water
1 tablespoon glycerine	Few drops perfume to scent

Wear gloves while using the caustic soda, as it burns. Melt the fat gently in a deep pan, then add the soda and water solution very slowly, stirring continuously and always in the same direction to avoid splashing. Add the coconut oil, glycerine and whatever you are using to scent the soap and continue to stir gently. Line a wooden seed-tray with a damp tea-towel, pour in the liquid soap, and store on thick newspaper in the airing cupboard for 24 hours. Cut it into blocks and store in a dry place for as long as possible before using; the more the soap can dry before being used, the longer it will last while being used.

Bath Oil

When you near the end of a bottle of favourite scent, leave a few drops in the bottom and half fill the bottle with almond oil. Leave long enough for the oil to absorb the scent before using in the bath, and make sure it is the concentrated form of scent, and not a toilet water, which will not be strong enough to scent the oil.

Flower, Herb and Spice Oils

Half fill a medicine bottle with petals, leaves or whole spices (lightly crushed) and cover with almond oil, cap lightly and stand in the sun or a warm place, for several weeks, until the oil is well scented. Flowers such as lavender, jasmine, pinks, damask roses and hyacinths are very suitable. Thyme, mint, lemon balm and rosemary make refreshing herbal oils, and mixtures of orange and lemon peel, cloves, coriander, cardamom, cinnamon and bay leaves produce exotically spicy oils.

Camomile flowers added to the bath refresh and revive. Tie a generous handful of dried camomile flowers in a handkerchief and put in the bath as the taps are running.

Talcum Powder

Talcum powder can be made to match your favourite scent very cheaply. Save an empty talcum container in which to store it. Mix 4 oz powdered French chalk with 1 teaspoon each of magnesium carbonate and calcium carbonate (precipitated chalk). Add a few drops of the scent and mix thoroughly, then leave to stand in a covered container for 24 hours before transferring it to the talcum container.

🌿 General Beauty Tips 🌿

To refine pores, put the grated rind of a lemon and 2 tablespoons bran into the foot of an old pair of tights, tying tightly to keep the mixture in. Steep this in hot water for a minute or two, wring out and sponge the face with it.

To Take away Spots and Freckles from the Face and Hands, with a secret not known unto many.

The sappe that issueth out of a Birch tree in great abundance being opened in March or April, with a receiver of glasse set under the boring thereof to receive the same doth perform the same most excellently and maketh the skin very cleare. This sap will dissolve pearl, a secret not known unto many.

Delightes for Ladies, 1660

Bathe sore, tired eyes with lukewarm water to which a pinch of boracic and some rose water have been added. Best of all, lie down with pads soaked in the solution over the eyes for about 30 minutes. Lukewarm China tea is also good for bathing eyes.

Milk smoothed over the whole eye area helps reduce puffiness

Rub your gums with crushed sage leaves every morning, to keep them healthy.

Add a few drops of vinegar to a glass of warm water and use as a mouth wash to freshen the breath (and chew parsley after eating garlic, as mentioned on page 161).

Keep a jar of bran in the kitchen and, after washing and drying your hands, rub them in the bran to keep them soft. Change the bran as often as necessary.

To remove the smell of onions from the hands, rub them with dry mustard before washing with cold water.

Very dirty nails and fingertips can be soaked in a solution of warm soapy water, to which a few drops of peroxide have been added.

Lemon juice is a good strengthener and cleaner. Use an orange stick dipped in lemon juice to clean under the nails after doing the vegetables or gardening.

The best long-term cure for brittle nails is regular buffing, using either beeswax or almond oil to rub into the nails beforehand. The friction helps the circulation in the nail area and so strengthens the nail itself, a much better solution than nail-hardeners, which are painted on and exclude the air from the nail, thus making matters worse.

Use yoghurt as a conditioner for fine hair. Apply it to the hair while it is wet after shampooing and rinsing, leave for 2 minutes, then rinse out very thoroughly.

Two rules for ladylike behaviour from *The Modern Woman* by Lillian Bradstock and Jane Condon, c. 1925:

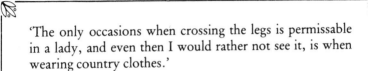

'The only occasions when crossing the legs is permissable in a lady, and even then I would rather not see it, is when wearing country clothes.'

'Be careful of scent when paying a country visit. Only the most bland of fragrances will blend with flowers and new-mown hay.'

⅍ *Custom and Superstitions* ⅍

'Wisdom gossip'd from the stars' — this phrase of John Clare's exactly describes the mixture of fact and fiction quoted in this short chapter, superstitious sayings which I couldn't quite bring myself to use as genuinely helpful hints in the other chapters, but which it would be a pity to omit.

There is a very fine line dividing fact from fantasy, and fantasy is almost always more appealing. For centuries, farmers have believed in the importance of doing various agricultural tasks according to the phases of the moon, but I was disappointed to learn recently that trials have been done at Wisley to test this, and have proved that the moon has little or no effect on growing crops, although it seems only reasonable to suppose that if the moon affects the tides, it must also affect growth.

I think few of us deny all superstitious beliefs. As a family we spend a lot of time in the summer looking for four-leafed clovers, even though we know that it is nothing more than a pleasant occupation for a warm afternoon. We are also very careful never to put new shoes on the table, easily done on returning from a shopping expedition. A friend in the village remembers the expression on her mother's face when, as a girl, she brought in a bunch of may blossom as a present. Her mother threw the flowers out of the back door, saying that there'd be a death in the family before the year was out (there was, but it was the expected death of an old grand-parent). Sayings like 'A green Christmas means a full churchyard' certainly have some sense in them. In the bitter winter of 1978/9, colds in our family were non-existent and even our oldest neighbours remained free from bronchitis. This winter has been very different, not very cold, and rather damp — colds, coughs and sadly one or two deaths have proved that piece of folklore more than superstition. The old rhyme

> 'If bees get out in February,
> Tomorrow will be rough and stormy.'

was proved right the other day, when bees buzzed in the crocuses one day, and were blown to bits the next; only those who knew the jingle were unsurprised.

Superstitions may be irrational, but they do add some sort of excitment to our modern lives, where most things can be predicted or explained by computer. An element of mystery is always welcome, the continuing popularity of horoscopes proves this, as do the piles of *Old Moore's Almanack* which appear every New Year in newsagents', alongside stacks of do-it-yourself magazines and car repair manuals. And *Old Moore* brings us back to John Clare's shepherd as he sits by his kitchen fire on a winter's evening and reads

179

Old moores annal prophecys
That many a theme for talk supplys
Whose almanacks thumbd pages swarm
Wi frost and snow and many a storm
And wisdom gossipd from the stars —
— He shakes his head and still proceeds
Neer doubting once of what he reads
All wonders are with faith supplyd.

The Shepherd's Calendar

❧ *The Moon* ❧

The phases of the moon play a very important part in superstition and custom.

Sow when the moon waxes
Weed when it wanes.

The moon on the wane,
Gather fruit for to last.

Thomas Tusser, 1638

Eggs were always put under the hen for hatching in spring,
during a waxing moon.

Pigs were killed during a waxing moon as it was thought that
if they were slaughtered during a waning moon the meat
would not keep and would shrink in cooking.

Bow three times to the new moon for luck.

It is unlucky to see the new moon first through glass.

Turn your money over in your pocket while staring at the new moon, so that it will multiply during the next month.

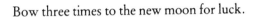 *The Calendar*

First Footing is an important custom still carried on in the North on New Year's Day. A dark man, carrying a piece of coal or wood (fuel), a penny (money) and a piece of bread (food), must be the first person to cross the threshold after midnight on New Year's Day, to ensure plenty of those three items for that household during the coming year.

The first pancake made on Shrove Tuesday would, in the Midlands, be thrown to the hens to ensure good laying.

Both potatoes and parsley should be planted on Good Friday, when the soil is free of Satan's power (but see page 115 for a more sensible approach). Parsley is reputed to go nine times to the Devil before it appears above ground, so if it is planted on Good Friday it might be saved at least one journey, and germinate more quickly.

In certain areas, it is thought to be unlucky to do any work at all on Good Friday.

Blackberries belong to the Devil after Michaelmas Day (September 29th), and so it is unlucky to pick them after that day. In fact, there has usually been a frost or two by then, so the berries will be past their best anyway.

Christmas puddings should always be made on the first Sunday in Advent, called 'Stir-up Sunday', and every member of the family should stir the mixture, and wish. This just sounds like an encouraging idea to enlist help with the beating of the mixture.

☙ *The Home* ❧

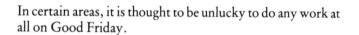

Always plant a house-leek somewhere on your house (on a porch-roof or in a cranny in the wall), to prevent the house catching fire or being struck by lightning. Culpeper classes it as a 'herb of Jupiter'.

White lines are painted round doorsteps in Northern England as charms against evil. This is still done, although white paint now replaces the unobtainable whitening.

Shoes belonging to the owners of a house would be thrown up into the rafters as the house was being built, to ensure happiness and prosperity.

Never put new shoes on the table, or the wearer will be dead within the year.

> See a pin and pick it up,
> All the day you'll have good luck,
> See a pin and let it lie,
> You'll want that pin before you die.

A long tail of wax down one side of the candle means death; a red dot at the top of the wick, a letter.

A dropped knife means a visit from a man; a fork, from a woman.

It is unlucky to kill spiders, as they provide all sorts of cures: cobwebs for cuts and spiders wrapped in butter to cure whooping cough, for example.

It is good luck to put on a garment inside-out, especially if it is remarked on by a stranger.

❧ *The Garden* ❧

Plant yellow flowers in your garden to protect yourself and your family from witches.

It is always a good sign when swallows and house-martins build nests in or near the house, and bad luck, therefore, to destroy their nests.

Always greet a single magpie courteously, because:

> One is for sorrow, but two for mirth,
> Three's for a wedding, four for a birth,
> Five for heaven, six for hell,
> But seven's the devil's own self.

Or:

> One for sorrow, two for mirth,
> Three's for a wedding, four for a birth,
> Five for silver, six for gold,
> Seven for a secret never to be told.

And there are many more variations.

Bees should always be told of a death in the family.

It is lucky to find nine peas in a pod.

To find a four-leafed clover is lucky, but only if the finder gives the clover leaf to someone else (he then receives the luck in exchange). It is odd how common four, five and even six-leafed clovers are becoming. Could it be a sinister warning against modern herbicides, which are breeding mutant varieties and ruining the fun of this superstition?

Corn dollies were made for each gable of the haystack, to protect the stacks against fire, lightning and any other misfortune.

❧ *Magic Trees and Plants* ❦

An elder tree near the house will protect it from witches.

Never dig up an elder tree, or burn one, because of their benign influence — they are pretty too, and make good wine and medicines. So far, I have had no bad luck from pruning elder — it is a vigorous grower and needs to be kept in check.

Elder juice was thought to be a powerful charm against warts.

Green elder-berries gathered on St John's Eve (June 23rd, the pagan Midsummer festival), protected the gatherer from witchcraft.

The rowan is another powerful antidote against evil, especially in Scotland, where bunches of rowan twigs were tied with red thread to the tails of the cattle to stop them being ridden by witches, and rowan boughs were nailed over barn and stable doors.

Passing a child through a split ash tree was supposed to cure hernia. I came across this odd piece of folklore first verbally, in Wiltshire, and then again when reading Gilbert White's *Natural History of Selborne*. I quote the whole extract without apology as it makes very curious reading:

In the farmyard near the middle of this village stands, at this day, a row of pollard-ashes, which, by the seams and long cicatrices down their sides, manifestly show that, in former times, they have been cleft asunder. These trees, when young and flexible, were severed and held open by wedges, while ruptured children, stripped naked, were pushed through the apertures, under a persuasion that, by such a process, the poor babes would be cured of their infirmity. As soon as the operation was over, the tree, in the suffering part, was plastered with loam, and carefully swathed up. If the parts coalesced and soldered together, as usually fell out, where the feat was performed with any adroitness at all, the party was cured; but, where the cleft continued to gape, the operation, it was supposed, would prove ineffectual . . . We have several persons now living in the village, who, in their childhood, were supposed to be healed by this superstitious ceremony, derived down perhaps from our Saxon ancestors, who practised it before their conversion to Christianity.

The ash was certainly regarded as a protection against evil; the keys would be collected, dried and used as charms.

Hyssop is a favourite bee plant, and was carried or grown as a protection against evil spirits. Fresh hyssop leaves were used to heal cuts. The mould grown on them produces penicillin, so it certainly has a scientific benign action, as well as a superstitious one.

Rosemary should never be bought, but always given. This is easy, as cuttings strike very readily. A sprig in a bunch of flowers brings good luck both to bearer and recipient, and bad luck to both if it is forgotten.

Holly should never be brought into the house before Christmas Eve, and should be out of it by Twelfth Night; it should not be burnt on a house-fire.

May-blossom should never be brought into the house. It is supposed to mean a death within the year. This is a powerful superstition, still very often quoted and believed in.

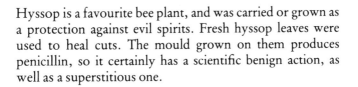 Love

The young girls whisper things of love . . .
And trying simple charms and spells
That rural superstition tells.

The Shepherd's Calendar

Peeling an apple in one unbroken strip, throwing it over your right shoulder and looking to see what initial it made on the ground was an infallible way of finding out who your lover was to be, as was twisting the apple stalk round and round while chanting the alphabet, to see at what letter the stalk parted from the fruit.

One of the many tricks for finding out who you were likely to marry was to write the names of the local boys on chestnuts, and roast them on All Hallows Eve. As the chestnuts shot out of the fire, there would be a scramble by the girls to pick them up and read the name.

✎ *Baby Charms* ✐

Pearls were considered an aphrodisiac, and childless couples were advised to sleep with a pearl ring beneath their pillow. To find a pearl in an oyster was thought to be a sign of conception, the pearl representing the fertilised egg in the womb.

To rock an empty cradle meant a baby on the way.

The eyes of new-born babies were touched with a licked finger to ensure good sight. Unhygienic possibly, but spit has always been considered a powerful charm, hence the spitting on palms before shaking hands to seal a bargain.

In Yorkshire, the traditional gifts to a new-born child were an egg, representing the necessities of life; salt, the luxuries; a silver coin, money; and a match or candle, to light the way to heaven.

In Cumberland, it is still the custom to slip a silver coin under the baby's head, presumably to ensure wealth. My daughter had several half-crowns given to her when she was first taken out in her pram. I hope they will bear fruit!

Also in Cumberland, a bowl of rum-butter and a plate of plain biscuits is set out for friends visiting a new baby. Rum-butter bowls are often found in antique shops in the area, and are sometimes of very fine china. The rum-butter itself was considered a good pick-me-up for newly-delivered mothers, and rum was rubbed on the baby's head to strengthen it.

The north door of a church would be left open during a christening, so that the Devil driven out of the baby by the holy water could leave by it.

It was thought safer to bite off the baby's nails when first they grew long enough, so that evil spirits could not get hold of the nail-parings to use in spells. Shakespeare throws extra light on this in *The Comedy of Errors*, when Dromio says, 'Some devils ask but the parings of one's nails.'

Coral was used for babies' rattles and teething rings because of its magic properties. It could indicate when a child was ailing because it would become pallid, and it was also thought to cure wind.

When milk-teeth fell out, they were thrown into the fire with a handful of salt, and this rhyme was chanted:

> Old tooth, new tooth
> Pray God send me a new tooth.

It is a Northern superstition never to lend an empty cradle, nor to return it empty. A small present was always put inside by both lender and borrower to ensure continuing fertility.

❧ Bibliography ❧

John Fitzherbert, *The Book of Husbandry*, c. 1550

Gervase Markham, *The English House-wife, Containing the Inward & Outward Vertues which Ought to be in a Compleat Woman*, 1649

The Inrichment of the Weald of Kent, 1675

Leonard Sowerby, *The Ladies Dispensatory*, 1651

Nicholas Culpeper, *The Complete Herbal*, 1653

Sir Hugh Platt, *Delightes for Ladies*, 1660

William Lawson, *A New Orchard and Garden, with the Country House-wifes Garden for Herbs of Common Use*, 1676

Hannah Wooley, *The Compleat Gentlewoman*, 1711

Richard Bradley, *The Country Housewife, and Lady's Director*, 1753

John Hill, *Eden, or, a Compleat Body of Gardening*, 1757

The Rev James Woodforde, *The Diary of a Country Parson*, 1758–1802

Hannah Glasse, *The Art of Cookery made Plain & Easy*,
  1784
Gilbert White, *The Natural History of Selborne*, 1789
W. A. Henderson, *The Housekeeper's Instructor*, c. 1790
Elizabeth Raffald, *The Experienced English Housekeeper*,
  1794
Mrs Rundell, *A New System of Domestic Cookery*, 1818
John Clare, *The Shepherd's Calendar*, 1827
Esther Copley, *The Housekeeper's Guide, or a Plain and
  Practical System of Domestic Cookery*, 1834
Stevens, *Book of the Farm*, 1844
Eliza Acton, *Modern Cookery for Private Families*, 1845
Charlotte Brontë, *Shirley*, 1849
Mrs Gaskell, *Cranford*, 1853
W. C. L. Martin, *The Pig: how to choose, breed, rear, keep,
  and cure*, 1860
Mrs Isabella Beeton, *The Book of Household Management*,
  1861
The Young Ladies' Journal (periodical), c. 1870
Dr Chase's Recipes, or Information for Everybody, c. 1870
The Rev Francis Kilvert, *The Diaries*, 1870–1879
Charles Elmé Francatelli, *The Cook's Guide and House-
  keeper's and Butler's Assistant*, 1888
The Ladies' Realm (periodical), 1904
Annie Butterworth, *The Manual of Household Work and
  Management*, 1910
*The Smallholder Year Book & Allotment and Garden
  Guide*, 1923
Lillian Bradstock and Jane Condon, *The Modern Woman*,
  c. 1925
Moira Meighn (ed), *The Little Book of Conceited Secrets*,
  1928